The **Artist** In Me

*An Incredible and Hilarious Journey with America's
Premier Christian Ballet Company*

Tim Dryden

Our goal is to provide high-quality, thought-provoking books that foster encouragement and spiritual growth. For more information regarding bulk purchases, other IP books, or our publishing services, visit us online or write to adam@ichthuspublications.com.

The Artist In Me: An Incredible and Hilarious Journey with America s Premier Christian Ballet Company
ISBN 13: 978-0692495469
ISBN 10: 0692495460
Library of Congress Control Number: 2015946418

Endorsements listed on the back cover are for entertainment purposes only. Any resemblance to real life authors or organizations were merely, *ahem*, coincidental . . . well, sorta— although we believe they probably genuinely reflect what might actually be said.

www.ichthuspublications.com

Printed in the United States of America

Soli Deo Gloria.

For my amazing wife Deana and our five precious children:
Mathias, Miriam, Micah, Wade, and Emma.

And for all of the pioneers of Ballet Magnificat, beginning with
Founder Kathy Thibodeaux and her husband Keith.

Barbara Bannister
Michael Cadle
Mary Cadle
Bo Denton
Honey Denton
Mamaw Denton
Mary Denton
Anna Carter Etheridge
Rick Faucher
Rose Faucher
Dianne Portier White
Lisa Roman
Greg Smith
Kyle Tucker
John Vandervelde
Karin Vandervelde
Cassandra Piotrowski Voborsky
Jiri Voborsky

Contents

Fore-
word

As a regular cast member on the "I Love Lucy" television series, I had the unique opportunity to participate in a behind-the-scenes look at the real Lucy and Desi, away from all the acting, the scripts, the cameras, the lights, and share in some personal moments with their entire family. For starters, I was always welcome to play with their children in any of their various homes in Southern California. Living the Hollywood experience was certainly a thrill, more exciting than the lifestyle I was accustomed to with my own family "over the hill" in the San Fernando Valley.

There were maids, cooks, and chauffeurs available at any hour to wait on us hand and foot. It was almost as if I stepped into Downton Abbey, and I loved it. Despite the glitz and glamour, though, I never thought of Lucy and Desi as being as wealthy or as extravagant as some of their neighboring celebrities and friends—folks like Dean Martin, Frank Sinatra, Jimmy Stewart, Jack Benny, and others.

Having grown up in the blue-collar town of Jamestown, New York, Lucy never seemed to forget her beginnings, nor did she treat those less privileged any differently from her own family. (Although, I suppose if I had any regrets or complaints, it's that I didn't get to ride more in either Rolls Royce sitting in the garages or the bright-yellow Ferrari, one particular car of Desi's I always admired). But the point is, I felt just as much at home and just as much a part of their family when I was with them as their own children. And being able to sit around the dinner table and talk like a regular family was always a treat for me and gave me a glimpse into some little-known tidbits about the iconic family.

There was one particular conversation we had that still remains with me vividly to this day. We were discussing some aspect of the entertainment industry, and Lucy seemed especially uncomfortable about her own comedic talent. "I don't really think I'm that funny," she stated rather matter-of-factly. It wasn't one of those comments where she was simply looking for reassurance and hoped someone would contradict her. She genuinely did not view herself as naturally funny, as she would say to us time and again.

Millions of viewers, however, even to this day, consider her to be one of the funniest actresses in television history. But Lucy's humor, as I would later discover as I grew older, was scripted, rehearsed, and perfected before it was recorded for the television audience. While she was certainly funny and could tell a good story, a portion of her comedic genius came from Hollywood script writers.

Tim Dryden, on the other hand, is one of those rare individuals who just *thinks* funny, seemingly all the time. He processes life and notices things "normal" people would never even notice—and if they did, they couldn't make the sort of comment that leaves you laughing uncontrollably or produces that refreshing moment of breathlessness. And the more you get to know Tim, the more you appreciate his quick wit. Even something as mundane as his reading a restaurant menu aloud will set you laughing.

The book you are about to read is unlike any book you have ever read. It's a delicious feast of hilarity seasoned with just the right amount of "cirrus stuff", as Tim would say. I've never had the heart to tell him that *cirrus* is a type of cloud—he means *serious* stuff. You'll enjoy savoring the taste of his humor and his incredible experiences as he recounts his journey through his life and his time with Ballet Magnificat.[*]

One little tidbit that didn't make it into the book—but remains one of my fondest memories while working together with Tim—happened in the Hoosier Dome in Indianapolis, Indiana. Tim's ability and *desire* to glad-hand anybody that is anybody to help promote our dance company can't be overstated (for which I was, and remain, always grateful). At times we were amazed, even embarrassed, at his boldness in approaching total strangers to get them to take notice of just how excellent and cutting-edge our ministry really is. Of course the ballet company needed the recognition he was seeking, and we all appreciated his zeal, but sometimes he got a little carried away. When his attempts to promote were ignored or rejected—always a hilarious display of events—we laughed until we cried because of his personality and how much we loved him. We always had "permission" to laugh because of how he would poke fun at himself in the melodramatic retelling of what happened. Even this one.

Gospel music icon and video producer Bill Gaither had called Tim and invited the company to participate in a week-long concert of notable musicians called, *The Praise Gathering*. In the course of organizing the event, Tim asked recording artist Steve Green if he would sing a certain set of songs to which choreography had been set, so that our company could dance for the 11,000 attendees that evening. Steve agreed to sing for the dancers (and what a brilliant performance it was!).

---

[*] Ballet Magnificat is an internationally-recognized arts organization founded in 1986 by Keith and Kathy Thibodeaux in Jackson, Mississippi. Ballet Magnificat is dedicated to presenting the gospel through the grace and majesty of ballet and the performing arts.

Tim, still brimming with confidence after scoring this connection with Steve Green, was walking down a long, dimly lit passageway inside the Hoosier Dome later that evening. He noticed a man approaching him, and, as he got closer, Tim was delighted to recognize that it was Bill Gaither himself. Not wanting to force Mr. Gaither to stop and chat in the passageway (Tim was way too discerning to do such a thing), he decided he would wait until Mr. Gaither was *just about* to pass him and simply say, "Thank you so much Mr. Gaither for inviting our ballet company to be a part of such an excellent event."

But all Tim managed to get out was, "Thank you so—" before Mr. Gaither threw his arms up to shield himself, backed against the wall for protection, and frantically increased his pace, all the while displaying a terrified look on his face which said something like, "I don't know who you are, but don't even *think* about robbing me, or I'll yell for security!"

Tim was crushed, not only for missing the promotional opportunity, but also for being mistaken by Bill Gaither for a common criminal. We laughed for weeks when he would imitate Mr. Gaither's fearful reaction. But that's who Tim is, and we cherish him dearly for it.

I miss Tim and his family tremendously now that they've settled in Virginia, but this book helps take away the sting by reliving our wonderful time together. I think you'll thoroughly enjoy the insights and amazing things that Tim shares in this book. Even though Tim's heart is in heaven, he has a way of bringing everything down to earth and seeing the funny in it. Tim, as it turned out, remains as close as my brother and the funniest person I have ever known—and that's saying a lot! I hope you enjoy his collection of stories as much as I have.

Keith Thibodeaux

WHADDAYA GET WHEN YOU PUT a bunch of Christian artists together from around the world, throw in a "Bubba" from the Deep South (that'd be me), add two or three kids for good measure, and push them to the brink of insanity by making them travel thousands of miles together on an over-crowded bus for weeks on end? No, this isn't the opening to a corny joke. It's my life story . . . well, part of it anyway. Or, perhaps a better way of answering the question is to say it is a recipe for some hilarious, crazy, unbelievable—yet true—stuff to happen.

Think about it. You've got a guy from Moss Point, Mississippi, who doesn't know how to spell "art", let alone "culture", trying to get a bunch of ballerinas and balledudes (if I just made up a new word, I hope Merriam-Webster takes notice and gives me my due credit) from point A to point B on a tight schedule. You've got a teenager from the Czech Republic (who sat behind the wheel of a car for the first time in his life one month earlier) checking the oil on your Greyhound bus, spraying some mysterious poisonous gas directly into the starter just to get the bus cranked up and running. Everyone with the exception of the driver is covered with blankets, because the heater doesn't work. You've got an Artistic Director who not only dances in every program—which is very rare—but who also begins each new day with a Snickers candy bar and a

Dr. Pepper, which is just downright odd. You have a male dancer who calls one of his seven children (yes, *seven!*) to wish him a happy birthday. You've got a ballerina nursing her six-month-old in the dressing room during intermission. Another dancer is severely nauseous and has been vomiting incessantly to the point of severe dehydration, so everyone gathers around and prays for God to heal her—and preferably *before* the program begins. You witness a ballerina from the North spend way too much time asking a waitress in Texas to explain exactly what she means by "red-eye gravy".

And all of this takes place *on the first day* of a three-week tour!

I love to tell stories and have told many people throughout the years about all the incredible, hilarious, and embarrassing experiences we shared together on the road. Over and over again, I was told, "You've got to write this stuff down." And so, I finally did. Difficult as it was, I've whittled the list down to the following thirty-something memories. A lot goes on backstage and offstage that remains concealed to the general public . . . until now. I'm forever thankful to have contributed a small part in such a big dream and will be doubly-blessed if these true stories cause you to laugh and consider the reality and grandness and goodness of God.

Let There Be Tutus

W HAT DO YOU MEAN, 'Start a *Christian* ballet company?' There's no such thing! Now that you've given your heart to Christ you're just gonna have to give up dancing and get a *real* job!"

Kathy Thibodeaux remembers hearing similar arguments when she felt God was leading her to dance to an overtly Christian song during the U.S.A. International Ballet Competition a few years before. She was told that she had an excellent chance of winning a medal for her country if she just wouldn't dance to that "religious" music. She decided to take her chances.

Winning the silver medal temporarily quieted a few of her critics, but this crazy idea of starting a Christian ballet company had some people wondering about Kathy's sanity.

She understood why it sounded odd to people, but she knew God had given her the vision. "I don't know the first thing about starting a ballet company, but I *know* God has put it in my heart, and he will provide whatever is needed."

Actually, she was somewhat aware of what it would take: an office space and headquarters, a rehearsal studio, excellent (and appropriate) music, and a choreographer—and that's just the beginning. Kathy also knew she would need someone to design and make costumes, as well as someone knowledgeable enough to call for bookings and coordinate the details of each program. And, of course, she knew if her dream was to be fulfilled, she would need several professionally trained Christian dancers who would be willing to relocate to Jackson, Mississippi (the cultural hub of the cosmos), and work for almost nothing, and at times, *absolutely* nothing. She also knew it would take money—lots of money. Again, she resolutely trusted God with all these seemingly impossible needs.

God proved that He would indeed provide everything necessary to fulfill the vision He had given to Kathy the very day after it appeared in the newspaper that she was resigning from her position as prima ballerina with the Mississippi Ballet. Dr. Newton Wilson, president of a small Presbyterian college in Jackson, phoned Kathy and offered her a small office for administrative purposes and a small dance studio, complete with mirrors and ballet barres—the essential elements of a studio. All she needed now was dancers! This was to be the first of hundreds of incredible ways our Sovereign Lord has provided for the company from the very beginning.

There is quite often humor—sometimes very subtle, but humor nonetheless—in how the Master Artist chooses to pull things together for his glory. Wouldn't you think he would choose a pastor of a charismatic, non-denominational church that met in a warehouse to offer studio and office space? There is at least one such church in Jackson. Instead, our infinitely complex and delightful Lord picked one of his so-called "frozen chosen" to fulfill the need for office and studio space for a *dance* company! And of course the price was perfect for the fledgling company—totally free! Though this alone was enough to convince Kathy that God was behind her vision, he sent even more confirmation in the days ahead.

A man named Greg Smith, who choreographed Kathy's medal-winning piece for the International Ballet Competition, had since moved to Portland, Oregon to help manage their regional ballet company. Kathy considered Greg a close friend and had come to respect him a great deal from an artistic standpoint. She felt he was the one to help her with all the administrative and artistic tasks that came with starting a dance company. She called him and enthusiastically shared her vision for a Christian ballet company. Then, the true purpose behind her call—she asked him to pray about moving to the Deep South to join her in this unique venture.

He listened carefully, but it didn't take long for him to flatly refuse her offer. He was finally making a decent salary and the people in Portland were extremely pleased with his work. His thanks-but-no-thanks response disappointed Kathy, but she continued to trust that the Lord would provide "that perfect someone" to assist her.

One week later she received a shocking phone call. On the other end of the line was the dejected voice of her friend, Greg Smith. Even though under his management, and through his newly instituted policies, the Portland Ballet Company was operating "in the black" (they had been on the brink of shutting down), they fired Greg Smith seemingly *for no apparent reason* (to him). There was, of course, a perfectly good reason. The Artist was in need of his services.

And so, Greg, along with Kathy, a handful of professional dancers from around the world, and a number of other folks who believed in Kathy's dream, embarked on a journey to create the nation's first Christian ballet company—to bring the "good news" through the performing arts.

I'm A Medical Doctor, Ma'am

M OSS POINT, MISSISSIPPI? he said in his best Southern drawl. Where in the [*expletive deleted*] is that?"

Everyone in the classroom roared with laughter at the instructor's obvious irreverence toward me and the Deep South.

Despite the instructor's insensitivity, I decided to play along and be a good sport. "It's about five miles south of Escatawpa, ya know, right next to Pas-ca-gooh-la," out-drawling his drawl.

More laughs, but most of them didn't realize I was joining in the banter. Someone commented that, "Nobody's ever even *heard* of Escatawpa!"

Duh.

It was the first day of a month-long school of instruction I had to complete in order to sell drugs—the legal kind, that is. The school was in Somerville, New Jersey, just a stone's throw from New York City. I was one of thirty-one students from all over the United States. Most in attendance were either microbiologists or ex-pharmacists. I was neither, and that soon became evident once I opened my mouth. My endearing Southern drawl made me the target of all kinds of comments, mostly rude ones. Maybe I was too sensitive, but it seemed like everybody from my instructor to my classmates to motel employees assumed, because of my Southern accent, that my IQ was lower than a snake's belly in a wagon rut. Consider a few more examples.

One evening after school I visited a new restaurant and was trying to decide what to order. So, I motioned for the waitress. "Excuse me, ma'am, what's the soup *du jour*?" I asked, exposing my adorable accent.

Not wanting to call attention to my obvious ignorance, she leaned over and whispered, "That's the soup of the day, honey."

Hmm.

A similar incident happened at the supermarket. The young lady at the cash register threw her head back and laughed in my face when she heard my accent. "Where *are* you from, man? Alabama? Arkansas?"

When I told her that I was from Mississippi, she smiled a sarcastic smile and shook her head, probably in disbelief that I not only knew where I was from, but that I could actually pronounce a four-syllable word like *Miss-i-ssi-ppi*. Then, with a smirk and the same condescending tone, she asked, "What in the *world* do you do for a living down there?"

I responded very politely and without hesitation. "I'm a medical doctor, ma'am—a brain surgeon, in fact. And what do you do for a living, ma'am?"

Before she could answer, and with her mouth still agape in surprise, I answered my own question. "Oh, sorry—*this* is what you do for a living, isn't it?"

Was my response kind? Not even a little bit. Did it feel good? Like hitting a game-winning home run! Lord, forgive me.

It's pretty amazing to me that the Lord would choose someone with my background and experience (and accent) to be part of a ballet company, of all things. I was born and raised in Moss Point, Mississippi, which is in the extreme southeastern corner of the state, about two miles north of the Gulf of Mexico and a few miles west of the Alabama state line.

My childhood was spent fishing, shrimping, oystering, camping, playing baseball, and mowing lawns. I don't think I ever spoke or even thought about the words *art* or *culture* until my late twenties, which is when I attended my first ballet performance. It so happened that I drove four girls to Atlanta, Georgia, to see *The Nutcracker*. At one point they teased me unmercifully for sleeping during the performance. I vehemently denied having fallen asleep, until they pointed out the huge wet spot on my light blue dress shirt where I had been drooling. So I lost consciousness for a few moments—can anyone really blame me? But I digress.

The next ballet I attended was a few years later in Jackson, Mississippi. I had gone to a restaurant to have lunch and had seen a poster with a picture of a ballerina and a scripture verse underneath with the words: ". . . *praise His name with dancing*. . . Psalm 149:3."

The advertisement was for Ballet Magnificat's second annual Christmas program. I had never heard of ballet with a religious theme; it piqued my curiosity, so I decided to check out the performance.

When I arrived, there were, by my count, some 300 people in the audience, which means there were about 2,000 empty seats. I sat alone near the back of the auditorium, because I thought it would be easier to make my escape if—I mean, *when*—I decided to leave. Little did I know that the next two hours would change the course of my entire life.

To this day—I still can't believe I'm about to admit this—but I truly enjoyed the dancing. Me. Of all people. "Bubba" from the Deep

South. But, before the snickers get too loud, in my defense, it took a while for me to stop thinking about the football game I was missing that afternoon on television. Eventually, I found myself actually getting drawn in to the program, even feeling a bit emotional. Thanks to the influence of my precious parents, Herbert and Neva Dryden, I attended church most every Sunday of my life. But I must confess there were only a few times before this performance that I had actually worshiped. And, as strange as it might sound, I had never felt this close to God! Forgive me if I sound a bit cornball, but it was truly an *awesome* experience.

This performance opened up a whole new world to me. I was impressed with the dancer's strength, athleticism, and grace. The aspect of the performance that, oddly enough to me, was most moving was the dancers' facial expressions. They were obviously having fun as they worshiped, and they seemed to be overflowing with authentic joy. I had never seen anything quite like it. At one point, a dancer named Michael Cadle talked about the God-shaped vacuum in all of us that only God can fill.

Michael had danced professionally with the Cincinnati Ballet before moving south with his wife Mary, also a professional dancer. I was moved by his genuine joy and love and his unrehearsed, heart-felt testimony. *How do these people get away with speaking so openly about God—and at a ballet performance?* I thought.

That afternoon at the city auditorium in Jackson, Mississippi, I felt like I experienced just a tiny taste of what heaven might really be like. As I watched, I realized that this was much more than just a spectator sport, because I was "dancing", too. After the program I found myself striding down the aisle of the auditorium to the stage. I wanted to find Kathy and tell her what I had begun to think about at some point during the program. I had met Kathy once before when she had accepted my invitation to speak at a weekly singles' meeting.

She saw me, but I wasn't certain she would remember my name.

"Hello, Kathy. Tim Dryden, that was a *great* program!"

"Awww! Thank you," she responded with her trademark smile. "To God be all the glory!"

"Kathy, I was really moved during the program. I feel like I worshiped in a way that I never have before. I feel like God is calling me to try to help with your ministry somehow."

"Really!?" she said, somewhat taken aback. "Well, what's your background?"

I responded, "Well, I've got a degree in administration, and I've been selling drugs—the legal kind—you know, pharmaceuticals, for about six years."

She smiled broadly and wanted to say something, but hesitated. Later, I found out she was thinking, *Administration and drug sales? How in the world is that going to fit into classical ballet?* She finally suggested we get together later that week to discuss the matter.

As I walked away from the auditorium to my company car that blustery afternoon, I felt an indescribable excitement deep within my heart, but I was also reeling a little from what just happened. *Did I really just talk to a professional ballerina about possibly going to work for her fledgling little company?* Surely not.

When we met the following week we talked about what role I might possibly fulfill within the company. I was certain it would be in the area of marketing and advertising for the company. After all, it bothered me that only 300 people attended the Christmas program. While I fretted about the paucity (betcha didn't think a Mississippi boy could come up with that word, did you?) of paying customers to each show, I could tell Kathy was *more concerned* with discerning if

God was calling me to this ministry than with anything I could offer. At the end of our meeting she prayed for guidance and suggested we pray about it. We agreed to meet again at some point in the near future.

A few months passed without much real direction, but I was still certain I was destined to work for the ballet. I shifted from praying regularly about whether or not it was God's will for me to leave pharmaceutical sales (because I was now convinced this was what he wanted for my life), to trying to logically figure out how this venture would be even remotely feasible. While it was good and wise for me to pray about the situation, it was not so good and wise for me to attempt to figure out how I could logically make it happen. There was nothing logical about it.

But, needless to say, I had some legitimate concerns. For instance, over the years, I had developed a habit of eating three meals a day (okay, so maybe four or five, but you get what I'm sayin'), wearing different clothes almost every day of the week, and finding shelter from nature. I enjoyed a good salary for years, along with a comprehensive medical, dental, and life insurance package. My pharmaceutical company provided me with a company car and even paid for my gasoline and any necessary repairs. I was living high on the hog! And I wanted to give that up? (I think I need to sit down just thinking about it all over again).

Anyway, as it would turn out, I spent more money entertaining physicians my last year with the company than I would earn my first year with Ballet Magnificat! In fact, my monthly mortgage payment alone was considerably more than the amount of any one dancer's salary at the time.

Wait just a minute! Was I losing my mind? That means even if they "paid" me (from the "love" offerings) *twice as much* as everybody else, that still wouldn't even cover my mortgage, let alone any other living expenses! Yes. It was confirmed. I was, in fact, losing *my* mind. God was planting in me just a small taste of *his* mind. He was giving me just enough faith to begin taking steps toward the unbelievable adventure he had in store for me.

Several more months passed. I ran into Greg Smith in the parking lot of First Baptist Church one Sunday (which reminds me, why does one never hear stories about Second or Third Baptist Churches?). I told him that I was still thinking about joining the ministry, but that I just didn't see how it was possible. He encouraged me to keep praying about it.

And so I did just that.

I was so groggy that I couldn't tell if I was dreaming the phone was ringing, or if it really was ringing. Either way, I shook off the slumber just enough to reach for the phone. *Who would be calling me at this ungodly hour on a weekday morning?*

"He-he-hello," I managed.

"Hey Tim, it's Richard." I recognized my district manager's voice on the other end of the line. He continued, "I'm at the Ramada Renaissance Hotel. Can you meet me here in half an hour?"

The anxiety in his voice made me nervous. "What's up?" I asked. "Is anything wrong?" He had never come to town unannounced, and he wasn't scheduled to work with me for another couple of weeks.

"Can you just please be here in 30 minutes?" Now he sounded annoyed. I figured I must be in trouble.

Richard was not a particularly friendly fellow. He wasn't the kind of guy you'd go fishing with, if you know what I mean (I'm fairly certain he didn't win the coveted "Class Favorite" award in high school, if that helps). Richard had just become my biggest nightmare.

I tried to calm myself on the way to the hotel, but I was worried. I took a deep breath, said a "flare-prayer" for courage, and knocked on his door.

He swung open the door while wearing an over-sized smile, one I surmised to be fake, and reached to shake my hand. He told me to sit down. He began explaining to me that he had flown into town because he wanted to see the expression on my face when he told me "the news". He began to review my track record with the company. He reminded me that I was ranked 5th in the nation in sales of our primary drug and that I had done an "excellent job" in all my continuing education classes since the original school in New Jersey. I was ranked 1st out of the 31 students in both verbal and written skills and received the "Top Student Award".

Richard couldn't contain the news any longer. "I'm here to offer you a promotion Tim! It's the offer of a lifetime—it couldn't be better!"

This is not what I was expecting to hear. I'm not exactly sure what I was expecting to hear—but I know this wasn't it.

I sat there, dumfounded, mouth gaping, still reeling from the news. He went on to explain that it was the much sought after hospital representative position in Kansas City, Missouri. He thought that I would be especially excited about the location, because he knew that I was a huge fan of George Brett, a professional baseball player with the Kansas City Royals at the time. The position would mean considerably more money, considerably less travel, and one more rung up the corporate ladder toward becoming a district manager myself one day. He stood up and held his hands up for me to give him a "high five".

What should have been one of the happiest days of my life was rather anti-climactic. A knot had formed in my stomach as big as a basketball. His face went from elation to deflation when I told him that

I had to pray about it. I explained to him that I had been considering leaving pharmaceutical sales to go to work for a ballet company.

"A *what* company?!" he shouted.

Uh oh. Now he was angry. I had awakened the sleeping bear, and he was not all too happy about it. Keep in mind, several district managers usually made appeals to their regional manager, on behalf of us lowly sales representatives, and then the regional manager decided who was to be promoted to this coveted position. The only problem was that Richard had "won" in convincing his regional manager that I would be best suited for the job in Kansas City.

"Did you say, '*Ballet* company'—like ballerinas and such?"

Before I could answer, he tried to calm himself with a deep breath, then continued. "Okay. How much have they offered you?" He reached for his pen.

"Richard, it's not about money. I know it sounds really crazy, but I feel deep in my gut like I'm supposed to try to help this little ballet company somehow. I'm sorry. I mean, I'm sorry you went to bat for me, I had no idea that . . ."

He slammed his legal pad down on the counter and angrily interrupted me. "So you're turning down this promotion?" he growled.

I realized that this would most likely be a crushing blow to my career in pharmaceutical sales should things not work out with Ballet Magnificat. Maybe this opportunity was God's way of protecting me from a bad experience with the ballet company. "May I please have a week to pray about it?"

"Pray about it?!" he shouted.

"I fly in this morning to tell you that you've been promoted to hospital representative, and you need to *pray* about it? Look, I know you're religious, and that's well and good, but you need to snap out of your daze, Tim, and think about your future! I'll give you two hours; that's when I have to leave for the airport."

"Two hours? Randy, you can't expect me to make a decision of this magnitude in two hours!"

"Two hours, Tim. I have to call Mr. Johnson (his regional manager) before I fly outta here. Be back here in two hours with your decision."

I went to a nearby restaurant, got a cup of coffee, and sat staring out the window, thinking through the insanity of what had just happened. Turning down a promotion as a hospital representative would be like digging for gold, finding a nugget the size of a cantaloupe, and covering it back up with dirt and walking away. Was it, or was it not, the wise thing to do to leave a solid future in pharmaceuticals? That was the question.

The answer was unmistakably *yes*. I smile as I type this, because my decision is so telling of the real power of God. There's no way I would have ever even *considered* being a part of a ballet company on my own. But the Artist knew the dance he had chosen for me long before I did.

And my, oh my, what an amazing journey it's been.

Vehicular Bliss

W HEN I LEFT PHARMACEUTICAL sales in December 1988 to join Ballet Magnificat, I had to return my company car (pretty cold-hearted company, huh?). I had no other car, but the ballet office was a pleasant ten-minute walk from the garage apartment where I lived. Over time, this brief workout became less and less pleasant, and catching rides to the grocery store, church, and other places was inconvenient, to say the least, especially in inclement weather. Bottom line: I *needed* a car.

A friend of mine loaned me her diesel Volkswagen Rabbit at times, but it was less than ideal for many reasons. For starters, it always drew stares, because it sounded more like a dump truck without a muffler than a personal automobile. The driver's door was permanently stuck shut so that I had to climb in and out of the vehicle through the passenger door. And the passenger door was permanently open, because there was no working latch, which meant I had to devise a way to hold it shut with a bungee cord attached to the gearshift. Another charming feature of the car was twenty or so strategically placed thumb tacks overhead, which prevented the upholstery from hanging down on my head or blocking my view. I always enjoyed the various expressions passengers made as they noticed my sweet ride.

My budget was less than $1,000, and after a couple of weeks of shopping, I found an absolutely gorgeous mud-brown Plymouth Horizon. Oh yeah, I was envied by all teenagers and young adults. Heck, it would go almost 50 m.p.h. and took just a shade under three minutes to attain that speed. The attorney who owned it wanted $800 for it and had agreed to my paying $100 per month until paid in full.

The body of the car was in pretty bad shape, and the interior smelled like a combination of dirty socks and wet dog, but it would crank and run, and the price was right, so I agreed to buy it. I was to meet the attorney who owned the car at 6 p.m. on a Tuesday night, test drive the car, make the down payment, and drive off into vehicular bliss.

But there was a big problem. The seller stood me up. Even though I let my team down by missing our weekly softball game to be there and waited until almost 7:30 p.m., he *never* showed up! I was bummed out and walked the 3 miles back home.

The next day I was working on our tour bus when a young lady walked up and asked if I had a minute to talk. I knew her name because she had once played on the varsity basketball team at the university I attended 10 years earlier, and I think we had officially met two or three years before, but we certainly weren't friends. Her name was Jan Barnett.

"You see that house right over there?" she asked.

I nodded.

"Well, right behind it is where my little apartment is, and some ladies from my church came over a little while ago to pray for me. We were praying about several things concerning my going on a mission trip in a few weeks.

"At one point, we began praying about what to do with my car while I'm away, and your name—Tim Dryden—popped into my mind.

I brushed the thought aside and tried to continue to pray, but again and again your name was coming to mind. I thought it very strange and tried to ignore it, particularly since you and I aren't really that close.

"But the thought wouldn't go away. I finally realized that the 'thought' was God speaking to my heart, telling me to check with you to see if you could use my car, or if you knew someone who could use it.

"When we stopped praying I told the women what had happened, and they agreed it was probably from the Lord. I thought I remembered hearing from a friend that you had joined this ballet ministry, so I thought I'd walk over and see if you needed a car."

My jaw literally dropped. I was dumfounded as I stood there, mouth agape. There is no way on earth she could know how I desperately needed a car. First, I explained to her that I had been without a car since returning my company car to the pharmaceutical company. I went on to tell Jan how, the night before, I was stood up by the owner of the severely ugly . . . I mean, aesthetically-challenged vehicle I was attempting to purchase. Second, I was amazed that a group of older Presbyterian women affirmed Jan in her belief that she heard from the Lord. It wouldn't have been quite so astonishing had they been of a more charismatic persuasion.

She joyfully exclaimed, "Well, praise God, there's our answer! *That s* why your name kept coming to my mind. You can use it, brother! I can't get it to you today, but in less than a week it's all yours for the duration of my trip!"

"That's *awesome*, but how do I . . . I mean, what do I need to do?"

She had this big, peaceful now-I-understand smile on her face. "Not a thing, brother. I'll just drive it over here and will hand you the keys in a couple of days. She turned and began walking back to her apartment.

I asked, "Well how long are you going to be gone?"

She kept smiling. "A minimum of one year, maybe as long as two years."

"A year! Maybe *two* years! Are you *kidding* me?" Tears began filling my eyes—the happy kind; the same kind of tears that frequently came when I knew God was providing for me. A car. A *free* car. Wow. By now she was out of earshot so I shouted to her. "By the way, what kind of car is it?" I didn't care if it was a riding lawn mower with a flat tire and a dead rat stuck in the engine. It was free and it probably wouldn't smell like dirty socks or a wet dog.

She laughed loudly as she turned and began walking backwards so she could shout a response. "It's a Ford Mustang . . . *convertible!*"

Microwave It, Girl!

O NE OF THE MOST INTERESTING things about traveling around the country has been the experience of staying in every imaginable type of accommodation and interacting with a myriad of personality types. Those who sponsor us put us up in motels occasionally, dorm rooms, apartments, but most often we were hosted by families in their homes. One particular night we shared a cramped mobile home with a single mom, three cats, a crying infant, and a partridge in a pear tree.

We especially savored those rooms we had to leave open so the cats could have full access to their fragrant litter box throughout the night. But, there were also many times we would be put up in really nice homes, even a few bona fide mansions. So I guess you could say it evened out . . . but it didn't really.

Just as an aside, there was, on more than one occasion, elderly couples who walked me and my wife to a room and said, "Okay we thought you would be comfortable in this room," only then to turn to me and say, "And sir, let me show you to your room upstairs." Huh?

Anyway, before I married my beautiful wife, another dancer, John Vandervelde, and I were being hosted in a beautiful home on the coast of Florida. The host couple were in their 60s and had only been church-goers for a few years.

The man had never really had any church experience, and the woman was a practicing Catholic for many years but until recently had no idea what she actually believed about God. She was incredibly excited about her new-found faith. Almost every sentence she spoke had something about the Lord in it.

"Good morning! Hasn't God blessed us this gorgeous day?! I was thawing out some sausage for you fellas but felt like the Lord wanted you to have bacon this morning."

Then there was the microwave versus conventional oven question, and God clearly said, "Microwave it daughter!"

Far be it from me to judge whether or not someone is *that* in tune with God but the fact remains, the woman was a bit wacky. She treated us royally and with the utmost respect, but John and I both concluded that the God of the universe probably wasn't that concerned with my midnight decision about whether to have a bowl of Cap'n Crunch or Froot Loops.

As the time neared for us to leave, I grew more and more critical of this woman and more cynical in my thoughts. *Why can't she be just a little more normal?*, I thought. Just before John and I were about to drive our bus from her home to where we were meeting the other dancers, she asked us if she could pray for our bus. I gave John this let's-tell-her-we're-in-too-much-of-a-hurry look, but John took her up on her offer.

She began normal enough: "Oh Lord, please be with this bus today, and keep it and the dancers safe." But then she laid her hands on the hood and that's when things got a bit weird. "Lord, keep this engine running smoothly, be with the transmission, keep the oil flowing through this motor, Lord."

Then she began to pray quite loudly in "tongues" (what sounded to me as pure gibberish) as she continued to lay hands all over the bus. John and I were slowly following her around the vehicle, and, all the while, I was *not* thinking Christ-like thoughts.

Suddenly she quit praying and stopped dead in her tracks. She began shaking her head very slowly while staring intently at one of the wheels. I looked at John and rolled my eyes, thinking, *What could she possibly be up to now?* Wagging an almost accusational finger at the driver's-side, outside rear wheel, she prophesied, "You're going to have trouble with that tire today. The Lord says that tire is trouble."

On the tag axle there are two tires side-by-side, and I pointed to the inside tire, and said, "*This* is the one we're going to have trouble with, right? This *inside* tire with no tread remaining, right? See what I mean?"

I began trying to "sell" her on the fact that the inside tire was as smooth as a baby's bottom, and could blow at any time.

"Because as you can see," I explained, "this outside tire you're pointing to has plenty of tread on it; it's the newest one." The outside tire was the one most recently replaced and was only a couple of months old.

Without taking her gaze off the wheel, she asserted confidently, "I can't help that it's the newest one, the Lord says you're going to have trouble with it today."

Sure.

We gave her and her husband a big hug and left. My hug was a hypocritical hug. I thought she was as crazy as a Betsy Bug. To my knowledge I've never seen a Betsy Bug. And I've wondered if there are intelligent Betsy Bugs as well as the infamous crazy Betsy Bugs, and exactly who determines their degree of intelligence, and by what criteria. Anyway, we met up with the other dancers and took off to our next destination.

Late that afternoon, a few hundred miles away from the unique-praying hostess, we heard what sounded like a gunshot, and the bus started wobbling. (You're ahead of me on this one, I'm sure). We had a bona fide, dyed-in-the-wool blowout. I almost tripped rushing off the bus to see if it could really be true. *It was.* There was a hole as big as a grapefruit in the very tire she had warned us about! I could *not* believe it.

Something else that was unbelievable? About three weeks later we were en route from Jackson, Mississippi, to Birmingham, Alabama, and we had another blowout. It was the *same* tire location. Unbelievably, a few weeks later we again had a blowout on the way to Louisiana. It was once more the same tire location! This time we had a mechanic check to see if there was something wrong with the *wheel* that was causing that particular tire to blow repeatedly, but he ruled that out.

We now had three different blow-outs, in three different states, on the very wheel location—the outside tag-axle wheel—that, as it turns out, our not-so-wacky sister in the Lord had warned us about. This experience taught me two important life lessons. First, our all-powerful God can and does speak clearly to his children. And second, don't judge wacky women.

The Dog Room

I'M ABOUT TO DESCRIBE TO you one of the more unusual experiences I ever had with a "homestay", the term we used to refer to hosts who kept us in their homes for the night.

Following a program in a southern state, the woman who sponsored us took me and my friend John Vandervelde to our room for the night. Let me say at the outset that she gave every appearance of being a perfectly normal woman. She had done an excellent job with all the details required to schedule a program; she had dotted all of the i's and crossed all the t's, and had done a superb job of promoting the event.

As we loaded our luggage into her car, she told John and me that she was going to take us somewhere where we didn't have to visit anybody, where we could have a little privacy. It was a camp house on a bayou. John and I welcomed such an opportunity. As we drove past her house, a lovely two-story home, she pointed it out, continued past it about a half mile, and turned down a dirt road. Approximately half a mile down the unpaved road we arrived at her quaint little camp house. It was surrounded by magnificent oak trees, and we briefly caught a glimpse through the beams of the headlights of the Spanish moss as it drooped effortlessly from the branches. It looked inviting and very picturesque, but as we stepped in the front door we noticed that she was taking unusually large steps for her size—as though she was stepping over something gross. To our utter amazement, when she turned on the light, we saw that she *was* stepping over gross stuff. A *bunch* of gross stuff!

You would not believe the trash that covered the floor of this otherwise picturesque camp house! It looked like something outta *Animal House*. Beer cans littered the floor, cigarette butts overflowed the ash trays; there was a little piece of rancid meat on the kitchen counter with a trail of happy ants, and the garbage cans were overflowing. It was a pretty disgusting sight . . . and smell.

I learned early on in our travels to accept with gratitude whatever accommodations were offered to me. I've stayed in some very modest places. I've slept on the floor, I've slept with dogs, cats, mina birds that didn't know when to shut up, and even a Vietnamese Potbelly Pig. (Kathy Thibodeaux can verify that the owners of said potbelly pig had potty-trained it by saying, "Pee-pee, poo-poo, *peppermint!*" repeatedly, rewarding the pig with a peppermint when it was successful. Crazy, but true story). I've slept on bottom bunks below snoring children, and I've never even considered refusing to sleep somewhere. But there's a first time for everything.

I wanted to very politely and tactfully and gently explain to her that I wouldn't let my Uncle Vester's hogs stay in this nasty camp house. "Uh, excuse me ma'am, I was just thinking that maybe—"

John knew what I was about to say and he interrupted me. He turned around and whispered to me, "Shhh! Remember, 'foxes have holes, birds have nests, but Jesus had nowhere to lay His head.'"

"Yeah, and hogs have pens, but I ain't staying in this dump!" I muttered under my breath. But I accepted his advice and watched in amazement as she showed us around the place, seemingly oblivious to its wretched condition.

It went from bad to worse. Neither of the beds had been cleaned or made up, and one of the sheets had a bright yellow spot as big as a Frisbee. Somehow the bedspread and sheets to both beds managed to find their way onto the floor. It was just plain nasty. The strangest part about it was that our seemingly sane hostess seemed utterly unware or unconcerned of the true circumstance of the house; she kept pointing out everything as if our accommodations were in pristine condition.

After she left, John and I decided to make the best of it. Not ten minutes passed before the "noseeums" arrived to wish us a hearty *hello*. Noseeums, mind you, are tiny little critters smaller than gnats, so you can't see 'em. But boy can you *feel* 'em; they began stinging us as if we had cursed their mother. We found some kind of unidentifiable salve in the bathroom we used to smear all over our arms and legs to keep the noseeums at bay.

We finally laid down to go to sleep and heard a noise in the wall that was undeniably rats chewing on wood. Everyone has a breaking point, and the rats were mine. I finally snapped. I stood up, tried to zero in on the spot where the rat was chewing, and slammed my fist into the wall. It worked, because we heard the rats scurry about. But then it stopped a few feet away and started chomping again.

"That's it, John. We're outta here."

And John agreed, so we jumped up and loaded our suitcases and proceeded to walk roughly the twenty miles (give or take a few) back to the woman's house to ask her if we could sleep in her home. Well, by now it's 1:00 in the morning, and as we approached the house, John was no longer quoting scripture. He asked me to do the talking.

I knocked on the sliding glass door, and we saw the lights come on upstairs, so she was obviously making her way down to us. When she got down to us she had her robe on and she opened the glass door.

"Oh my goodness, what's wrong? How can I help you?"

"Well, you know we were trying to go to sleep and the noseeums were getting us and then a rat started chewing in the wall, and we just couldn't sleep so we were wondering if you might allow us to sleep here tonight."

She answered with genuine compassion, "Well of *course* you can come here and sleep; you can sleep right here in the dog room." It was then that we noticed in the tiny room in which she was standing, there was a fold-out cot leaning against the wall and a doghouse labeled "Tuffy," with its canine occupant peering at us sleepily.

We hoped Tuffy, a basset hound with sad eyes and long ears, would be hospitable. John needed the cot because he's the dancer, so I curled up on the floor with Tuffy. Seriously.

The night finally passed and the rest of the dancers had been invited to a scheduled 10 a.m. send-off brunch prepared by our hostess. About 10:30, our hostess showed up with some 9 bags of groceries to *begin* preparing food for the brunch. This was not good, because it would put us severely behind schedule. And the schedule was extremely important to keep, because we always requested 10 volunteers to meet us on arrival at the next destination, at a precise time, to help us unload equipment and set up critical lighting and sound equipment, costumes, and flooring, in addition to a number of other duties. This assistance is essential for the dancers who, in addition to helping with the set-up, would also endure a two-hour class and warm-up, followed by a two-hour program, and a one-hour tear down and load up. It is a much more physically demanding daily routine than one might think.

Our blissfully unaware hostess began cutting fruit in the kitchen and had placed a large ham on the bone in the middle of the kitchen table. The dancers were visiting with each other and remaining patient as we all realized the brunch was going to become lunch, and we would be departing for Miami much later than planned. I was not as patient and kept coming to the kitchen, offering to help as the dancers had tried, in an effort to speed along the process.

As I walked in to check on her progress, she had her back to the table and was washing something in the sink. Tuffy had shown up. You know how dogs will stand on their hind legs and put their front paws up on a table and eat anything they can reach? Well, that's not what this dog was doing. Tuffy was more advanced in his efficiency and technique. He was completely *on top* of the table, positioned over the ham (his tummy was touching the ham) and was chowing down on his delicious feast. He was smacking more than the rat was the night before, and no doubt the flavor of the ham topped the wood in the wall of the camp house.

I said firmly, "Tuffy get down off that table! Get away from that ham!"

And, meanwhile, Sherry didn't even turn to look from her position at the kitchen sink. So I loudly slapped my hands and said even louder, "*Git* down off that table!"

That dog looked up at me with those sad eyes and a big ol' piece of ham hanging out of his mouth as if to say, "Who are you to tell me to get down off this table."

Finally the woman turned around, saw Tuffy and the half-eaten ham, and, with a big smile, exclaimed, "Tuffy, you little rascal! Now I'm going to have to wash *every* piece of that ham!"

Yes she really said that. So, being the kind-hearted individual I am, I went around and whispered to all the dancers to stay clear of the ham.

Bless His Chubby Little Heart

E IGHT WEEKS?!" I SHOUTED. "The world as we know it could be *gone* in eight weeks!"

It was the night before the company was to dance on The 700 Club, filmed by the Christian Broadcasting Network (CBN) in Virginia Beach, Virginia. The CBN staff had treated us like royalty since our arrival. They had fed us a phenomenal five-course meal and had put us up for the night in their plush luxury 5-star hotel. The night before our accommodations had consisted of the extremely un-plush bunks on our tour bus. We had travelled through the night following a program in Jacksonville, Florida in order to make it to the coast of Virginia on time.

Just after we had taken a dip in the pool at the Founder's Inn, I approached John, who was my close friend and our company minister, about something very confidential. I explained to him that I had been having "really weird feelings" toward one of our dancers, Deana Horner, for several weeks. Of course, he asked me to expound on what I meant by "weird feelings". This was a big deal, because dating was not allowed at all among company members. Nor was having "weird feelings" toward a young, pretty dancer.

I explained that I thought it was real love—like romantic love. I explained that even though she was so young, I wanted to ask her out when we got back home from this tour. I braced myself for the barrage of oncoming verbal assault missiles about to be fired in my direction. I had made up my mind that I was going to stand my ground, no matter how many plausible arguments he shot at me about the utter absurdity of a man my age being interested in a girl that young (I'm 13 years older than Deana). I *really* wanted to spend some time with her.

John surprised me in two ways. First, he said she might feel the same way about me (that didn't seem altogether plausible), and second, he suggested we pray about it for a couple of months first.

Our age difference was only the tip of the proverbial iceberg regarding our differences. Deana is an extremely calm person. I'm an extremely hyper person. Deana is soft spoken and fairly quiet, while I tend to talk . . . a *lot*. My dad says, "Ask Tim what time it is, and he'll tell you how to make a watch." A friend of mine from my hometown metropolis of Moss Point, Mississippi often complained that I could "talk the horns off a billy goat." Deana is gentle and patient; I'm blunt and impatient. She's from Pennsylvania, and I'm from Southern Mississippi. I grew up peeling shrimp and shucking oysters. She grew up taking 18 hours of ballet classes each week. And the list goes on.

The prayer that John recommended that we pray is one of the main reasons this story is included in this book. All would-be relationships would do well to start where we started.

John said, "Let's pray that God would either take away your desire for her, or that He would give her a desire for you."

My brow furrowed as I contemplated his counsel. Regardless of how the Lord would choose to answer this prayer, I would be put out of my misery. Things would be better. He would either birth in this precious girl a desire to spend time with me, or take away my yearning to spend time with her. Hmm. That sounded good.

So we committed to pray fervently about the situation for eight weeks. John and I almost always roomed together on tour because his wife was home with their 7 children, and I was single. We prayed daily that God would either take away my desire for her or give her a desire for me.

The day finally arrived. Eight incredibly long weeks had passed. The company was touring in Texas, and all of us were being housed under one roof just outside Dallas in the small town of Flower Mound. A local pastor was on a trip to Europe and had allowed us to crash in his large home for a couple of nights. John and I decided it was time to pop the question about a potential date, but I needed to talk to Kathy first, since she was the Director of the company. So I explained to Kathy my intentions and how John and I had been praying about it for two months.

"I knew it—I just knew it Tim," she said. "I sensed that this was coming."

Her reaction surprised me because I thought nobody in the world had even a vague idea as to how I felt about Deana, except John.

"Really?" I asked. "Has it been that obvious?"

"Oh, no, not really. I mean, you haven't been acting weird or anything. I guess I just felt deep inside that something was up. I think you ought to talk to Deana about it."

Hallelujah! The light had finally turned green. I had gone through the proper channels and received the "go ahead" from John, Kathy, and most importantly, God. It was late, so I decided to wait until morning.

No matter what the outcome, things would probably never be the same again. If things didn't turn out the way I hoped, it would probably be a long time before she would feel free to cry on my shoulder. Or ask me to pray for her. Or just talk. No matter how hard we would both try to prevent it, our relationship would almost certainly be strained for some time. Maybe forever. But if things *did* work out, well, I couldn't even imagine how great that would be.

The next day finally arrived. It was time. I was ready to talk to her. I began looking through the house and couldn't find her anywhere. As I headed for the back door to look outside I saw her through the window. I stopped and just stared (but not in a creepy sorta way). That beautiful picture of her is indelibly etched in my mind's eye. She was lying in a hammock with her Bible propped up on her chest, reading God's word.

I walked up to the hammock. "Hey Deana, how are you doing today?"

"Oh, hey Tim. I'm doing great. This hammock is so comfortable! What are you up to?"

(It surfaced later that Deana thought I was going to correct her for taking too long to do her job in the set-up).

"Well, I just wanted to talk to you about something, but I can wait until you finish your quiet time." She left her Bible open but laid it down on her chest.

"Oh, it's okay, this is a good time. I can finish reading this in a few minutes."

I gave it my best shot, but I couldn't spit it out. I looked down at the ground and cleared my throat that fake way people do when they're stalling for time trying to figure out what to say next. I could feel the perspiration forming just above my top lip and on the palms of my hands. I was ridiculously nervous.

The silence was shattered by the roar of a motorcycle as it sped around the corner of the house and headed directly toward us. We watched as the pastor's son, barely a teenager, zipped up to the hammock and skidded to a stop. He was staying with a neighbor while his parents were away.

"C'mon! You wanna ride?" he motioned for Deana to hop on with him.

And she did!

I stood in disbelief, with my mouth agape, as she hopped out of the hammock and onto his dirt bike and together they sped off. Grass and dirt kicked up onto my blue jeans as they roared off. Surely this *must* be a sign. God sent locusts to Pharaoh, handwriting on the wall to forewarn an evil king, and now he sent a kid on a dirt bike as a sign to me.

I remained motionless, incredulous by what just happened. I didn't even brush the dirt off my pants. To say I felt like such an idiot would be an understatement. Sure, like she was really going to want to go out with me. Certainly the great Rescuer had intervened to protect me from what would have been a very embarrassing experience. Before I could wallow any further in self-pity and negative thoughts, the bike turned around and headed back toward me.

Deana hopped off the motorcycle as quickly as she had mounted it, and jumped back into the hammock. "That was fun! That thing goes pretty fast. Now what was it that you want to talk to me about?"

I hemmed and hawed for what seemed like forever, then finally asked her if she would consider the possibility of praying about maybe going out with me when we returned home from that tour. There. I finally spit it out.

Her bottom lip started quivering. Tears welled up in her big brown eyes. I didn't want to make her cry just because she didn't want to humiliate me or hurt my feelings; it was okay if she said no. I thought she was probably saying to herself, "Bless his chubby little heart; I have no interest in going out with him."

"Tim, I've been praying for several weeks now that—" she paused to sniff and wipe the tears away. "I've been praying that the Lord would either take away the feelings that I have for you, or that He would give you the same feelings for me."

What?! Is this really happening?! Did I just hear that correctly?!

At first, I just stared at her—like a dog when he hears a high pitched sound and turns his head sideways. Did she really say what I thought she said? "Are you serious?"

She nodded and smiled through her tears.

Wait just a minute . . . "Deana, have you discussed this with John Vandervelde?"

"John?!" I haven't breathed a word of this to *anybody*—not even my mom. Why do you ask that?"

It was at that precise moment that I realized that the Master Artist had skillfully placed it in both of our hearts to pray toward the same end, and I *knew* I was looking into the eyes of my future wife. I found out later she was thinking the same exact thing (except for the future wife thing; she was thinking future husband).

One of the delightful mysteries of God is that He makes choices, beautiful, creative choices. I'm eternally thankful to the Artist for choreographing this life-altering turn of events. He arranged my marriage. He hand-picked a Pennsylvania flower who was born 1,000 miles north of where I was attending junior high school at the time. He picked her to be *my* bride. Wow. He made the absolute *perfect* choice. But then, He always does.

My Pennsylvania Flower

ABOUT THREE MONTHS after I graduated from college with a degree in Public Administration, and a minor in Political Science (which, combined, are about as valuable as a degree in Archery), a nine-year-old girl named Deana Horner had a dream come true. She finally would be joining her two older sisters for ballet classes at a dance school in their hometown of Harrisburg, Pennsylvania. While her sisters enjoyed taking ballet classes, Deana was *consumed* with dance—her greatest dream was to one day become a professional ballerina.

Did her family and dance teacher take her seriously? Not really. It was the dream of scores of thousands of young girls. Their moms take them to see *The Nutcracker* every year around Christmas time, and a dream is born. But Deana had the added motivation of wanting to imitate her older sisters.

Her sisters and others at the dance school affectionately called her "Deana the Dynamo", because she seemed to have inexhaustible energy—even for a nine year old. She would take an hour class with those in her age group, then the teacher would allow her to take her sister's 90-minute class as well. This was against the school's policy, but she was basically taking the class anyway off to the side of the dance floor. After all, her teacher knew Deana had to be there for the time anyway to wait on her parents to come pick up all three of them.

Soon, Deana's hard work began to pay off. Her technique ranged from better than average to excellent for a girl her age. She was chosen to play the part of Clara in *The Nutcracker* for the first time when she was nine years old. It was a very exciting time for Deana and further solidified her dream to be a dancer "forever".

Her training schedule at the Central Pennsylvania Youth Ballet in Carlisle, Pennsylvania was incredibly demanding. Throughout her high school years, Deana endured the strict Russian Vaganova training for three grueling hours each day, six days a week. If she missed a class, she had to make it up. Her family also had to pay a price for her rigorous training. Not only did her parents have to pay for the classes, but they had to drive her 50 miles every day.

One weekend during her 10th grade year, Deana attended a special program offered by her youth group at church. At one point the guest speaker taught the importance of putting God first in *everything*. They emphasized that Jesus had to be our priority, our focus, our very life, and that we could allow nothing to block our relationship with Him. Simply put, nothing can be more important to us than him.

To illustrate this point, a large wooden cross was brought in and erected near the front of the room. A small piece of paper was passed out to each person in the group. The speaker then told them to write down anything, *anything* that might be standing between them and God.

Tears came to Deana's eyes. She knew God was speaking to her heart. At that point in her life, ballet itself meant more to Deana than her relationship with the Lord. But she was afraid that if she put Him first, and her dancing second, that somehow ballet would be taken from her completely. Deana decided to nail her ballet to the cross—literally. She wrote the word "ballet" on the little slip of paper and made her way to the front of the room. She picked up the hammer and nail, took a deep breath, and "crucified" the love of her life. This overt action symbolized an inward de-throning of ballet, and was an acknowledgement that Jesus Christ is Lord, Boss, King.

Although this proved to be an important turning point in Deana's life, the Lord didn't take away her love for ballet. She continued to train throughout her high school years, with the goal of one day being accepted into a professional company. In September of 1988, her childhood dream was realized. The Pittsburgh Ballet Theatre offered Deana her first professional contract. She was so excited! Leaving the security of the only home she had ever known, she packed her bags and moved four hours west of her hometown to Pittsburgh.

She was given a 40-week contract, pointe shoes faster than she could break them in, and the opportunity to dance with much more experienced dancers. It was fun travelling by plane to dance in different cities—and being paid for it. But mixed with the excitement was a hollow feeling that, at first, Deana didn't quite understand. She was doing what she had always wanted to be able to do. But something was missing.

That "something" was spending time with others who had put God first in their lives. None of the other dancers—not one as far as Deana could tell—were believers. Drug use and sexual promiscuity was commonplace, and it seemed like almost everybody was ruled by their love of dance, or self, or both. She tried to immerse herself into the Bible, but after several months of being surrounded by rampant godlessness, Deana was becoming increasingly discouraged. If this was what being a professional ballet dancer was all about, she was ready to give it up altogether.

She had shared her feelings with family and friends, and asked them to pray for her to know what to do next. After one year of living out her "dream," she was considering the possibility of dropping out of dance entirely. Then, one weekend, while home in Harrisburg for a visit, the Choreographer of life began to orchestrate a chain of events that would change Deana's life forever.

A close family friend and former youth worker in Deana's church, Jane Prestosh, called her and gave her some very interesting information. Two years earlier she had read an article about the Christian rock band, David and the Giants. The article had explained that the drummer, Keith Thibodeaux, was married to a ballerina who had founded a Christian ballet company in Jackson, Mississippi. Jane asked Deana if she would be interested in finding out more about this unique company. Deana was very interested, so in February of 1989 Jane arranged a conference call with Ballet Magnificat. At the time, there were only two non-dancing staff members, an ex-Marine from Hawaii named Jeff Bieber and me. Jeff answered the call.

Deana asked all of the usual questions. "Do you offer a 40-week contract?"

The answer was no.

"What's the starting salary for corps dancers?"

Jeff explained that none of us were paid by salary, but based on our need for any given month, *and* according to how much "love" had been in the "love offerings" lately (translation: you will be paid very little, if anything).

"Do you provide health insurance or worker's compensation?"

Jeff tried to suppress a chuckle, then explained to Deana that they could not offer either benefit.

Jeff briefly touched on the most important criteria for becoming a part of Ballet Magnificat—the call of God. Deana knew that he was right. Compared to other professional ballet companies, the conditions under which these dancers worked were downright ridiculous. But these same, almost laughable conditions, are what the all-wise Choreographer used to draw Deana *to* the ministry, rather than scare her away. Deana has said that she realized these dancers must be the real deal. She knew they must be driven more so by the desire to exalt the Creator of dance, rather than dance itself, or worse still, themselves.

It was during this initial phone call that Deana began to feel the call of God on her life, and she began to understand why she had trained so hard for so many years. But the big question to her was, "How in the world do they combine classical ballet with worship?" She also wondered about the quality of dancers who would join such a company and how they survived financially.

The answer to both issues came only hours after her flight landed in Jackson, Mississippi, in March of 1989. Kathy Thibodeaux had requested that she travel to Mississippi both to audition and to spend a week "getting to know us, and letting us get to know you." To Deana, this was another extremely out-of-the-ordinary request made by what Deana was recognizing more and more as an extremely out-of-the-ordinary ballet company.

The following is Deana's own account of her first few hours in the Deep South:

I guess I was expecting to see rows of antebellum homes everywhere and everybody to speak with accents like the characters in Gone With The Wind. *I thought everybody and everything would look more rural—I wasn't expecting it to be so commercially developed. I had never been that far south or west, so the entire culture was quite different to me. I definitely wasn't expecting the colorful character who picked me up at the airport!*

I had been instructed to be on the lookout for a young Hawaiian woman, who happened to be nine months pregnant. But as I exited the plane there was nobody of that description in sight. Before I had time to start worrying, a man with a big smile approached me and asked, "Are you Deana Horner? I can tell you're a dancer by the way you walk."

To this day, I don't know how he picked me out of the crowded group of passengers coming off that plane. At the time I remember thinking how embarrassed he would have been if he had "picked" the wrong person. Now that I know him, it doesn't surprise me at all that he picked me out of that crowd—he's very, very observant. And, looking back on it, he was probably hoping that I was the wrong person, just so he would have another funny story he could tell.

He was a very different kind of person. He didn't look poverty stricken (though at the time he really was), and he did speak with a deep thick, Southern accent, but not like the characters in Gone With The Wind. He described everything in funny ways. Now that I think about it, he described things that no one else would even bother to describe. Somehow, though, he made me feel like we had been friends since grade school.

He insisted that he carry my luggage, and on the way to his car he asked me to sit down for a moment. We sat down, and he said that there was something he had to tell me. My heart sank. I thought he was going to tell me that they had filled the position with another dancer. Instead, he started explaining in great detail about the horrible condition of his car. He explained something about how it smelled, then told me that the driver's side door was permanently locked, the passenger side door wouldn't latch so it was permanently open, and that he had put thumb tacks in the overhead upholstery to keep it from drooping down on my head. I was so relieved that his car was the only problem.

As we drove out of the airport he asked if he could pray for me. It was so encouraging and comforting. It was as though he knew exactly how I was feeling, and even what I was thinking. Then he practically forced me to memorize a scripture that has come to mean more and more to me through the years—Jeremiah 29:11-13.

Two hours later we arrived at the First Baptist Church of Selma, Alabama, where the company was nearing the end of their program. We hurried inside and took a seat on the back row as they were finishing up one of the first songs ever choreographed for Ballet Magnificat, Sandy Patti's, "Morning Like This". My eyes were riveted to the dancers (Rick Faucher, John Vandervelde, and Mary Cadle), as they beautifully portrayed the biblical account of Peter, John, and Mary celebrating their discovery of the empty tomb.

I had no idea that the Southern guy sitting next to me, the one who picked me up from the airport two hours earlier, Tim Dryden, would one day be my husband. I also had no idea that I would be "married" to this little dance company from Mississippi for at least the next 10 years! I vaguely remember Tim asking me if I could dance like them, but my eyes were glued to the stage.

Then Kathy Thibodeaux danced her silver medal winning solo to Sandy Patti's, "We Shall Behold Him". It was during that piece that I realized that this is what God had been preparing me for all these years—to dance for him.

After spending several days with the company in the studio and in their homes, I returned to Pennsylvania. I wanted to discuss how I was feeling with my parents, and receive their counsel, but my mind was practically made up. I believed God's call on my life was to move to Jackson, Mississippi, and dance for him. Did Kathy and the other members feel the same way? I wouldn't know for another week.

Several weeks earlier I had sent a video of myself to the Nashville Ballet, and two days after I returned from my trip down south, the artistic director called me. He offered me a contract solely based on the video I had sent. One almost always has to audition in person to receive a contract offer. This put me in a faith-testing dilemma. If I accepted his offer, and then received an invitation from Kathy, I knew I'd leave Nashville and head for Mississippi. On the other hand, if I refused his offer, and Kathy didn't invite me to join Ballet Magnificat, I would miss out on both opportunities.

I explained to him that I was leaning strongly toward going with a newly formed, small company down in Mississippi. He wanted to know if my decision was based on money, implying that he could match the offer. I told him that I had not even been offered a position yet, and if they did invite me, there would be no contract, no benefits, and very little money. I think he concluded that I must be a quack and gave up on me. That didn't matter to me much, but what did matter to me a great deal was whether Kathy and the others wanted me to be a part of their unique little company.

Several days later Kathy called Deana and invited her to be a part of Ballet Magnificat.

She arrived in May of 1989, we were married in September of the following year, and our son Mathias was born in September of 1991. In the early months of her pregnancy, we had to stop the bus on several occasions due to her violent episodes of morning sickness. One such stop was in the wee hours of the morning in the desert of Southern California, near Blythe.

I had been driving for hours, and dancer Michael Cadle had taken over so I could get some sleep. Michael pulled the bus over and stepped outside with her so she wouldn't have to throw up all alone in the desert. I mean, he didn't join her in barfing, he was just out there with her. As soon as he stepped down off the bus, he exclaimed "Wow! You guys ought to see all the stars—it's incredible!"

Almost everybody disembarked to check out the stars, while Deana was actively being sick only a few feet away. I rolled out of my bunk to see what was going on and was told that Deana had to throw up, and everybody got off the bus to check out the stars. I didn't really understand, I guess maybe I was still too groggy. I do remember, however, feeling bad for Deana. It was bad enough to have to barf in the desert, but couldn't she at least have some privacy?

Fast forward to when Deana was five months pregnant with our first child, Mathias. That is about the time when we shot our first video, *Symphony of Movement*. She said sometimes when she had to do turns her belly reminded her of a washing machine off balance. You know, when all the clothes shift to one side. I don't know which is more remarkable: that Kathy encouraged her to keep dancing even though she was going to have a baby, or the fact that Deana travelled to 18 states and performed in 40 programs while she was carrying our son. Little Mathias was on 40 different stages before he was ever even born! Most of you who know us personally will agree, even more remarkable is that God would bless me so incredibly much with a wife so beautiful and strong.

Mathias began touring with us when he was just eight weeks old. The little fellow travelled to 21 states with us during his first year of life. Many times Deana would actually nurse him during the programs at intermission. On more than one occasion we had to extend the intermission so she could finish feeding him. Four years later we had our second child, a precious, gorgeous, baby girl we named Miriam, who also began touring the nation at 8 weeks of age.

Deana's strongest attribute has probably been her attitude of consistent joy through the years. Objectively speaking, she has the most beautiful smile in the universe. Folks across the nation have encouraged her by telling her that it's evident that she's not *just* doing ballet, but that she's worshipping her Savior.

Deana danced for the Artist's glory for about 12 years . . . well, come to think about it, that's not totally accurate. It turns out all those early years of training were also for the Lord. From the standpoint of strengthening her, and preparing her for ministry, even the secular roles she did prior to Ballet Magnificat were done ultimately for His glory.

Deana's Mom, Joyce Horner, told me once that while she was pregnant with her, "Deana was very, very active, and had lots of movement." Knowing the Artist, He probably had her do a pirouette or two in her mother's womb—just for him!

Heaven-Sent Honeymoon

T HE CALL CAME FROM Harrisburg, Pennsylvania, on an incredibly hot afternoon in July. Deana and I had been sweeping the floors and scrubbing fixtures in the modest little two-bedroom, single-bath garage apartment which would become our first home following our upcoming wedding. Long-time family friend Jane Prestosh was on the other end of the line. Jane was the person who first told Deana about this unique ballet company down in the Deep South.

"Hello Tim, this is Jane, is Deana there?"

"Oh, I'm sorry, you just missed her; we've been cleaning all afternoon."

"Well, let me explain things to you Tim, and you can tell Deana. Mike (her husband) and I aren't going to be able to be at your wedding and we're *sooo* sorry! I had already purchased tickets to fly to Hawaii to see my uncle, and there's just no way to undo all my plans. I hope you guys can understand?"

I wanted to relieve her of any anxiety. "Listen, don't worry about it *at all!* We would never expect you to change those kinds of plans to attend a 45-minute wedding ceremony. We'll miss seeing you, but we'll probably be back up in Pennsylvania at Christmas, and we will definitely visit you then."

"Let me ask you a question, Tim," she continued. "I was thinking about what we could give you two for a wedding present, and I was wondering if you think Deana would like it if we provided all the greenery for the sanctuary for your wedding day."

I knew her well enough to know that she would probably go all out and go to a great deal of trouble and expense if I approved of her plan. Deana and I were getting married *during* an upcoming tour which would take us up the east coast into Canada. We were stopping in Harrisburg on our way back to Mississippi long enough to do a program, and get married, then we were boarding the bus and heading home. It was going to be a relatively small gathering of some of our friends including all of the dancers. In fact, some of the dancers were going to actually dance in the ceremony, and all of the dancers would join Deana and me in the front of the church and sing a couple of songs. I had to be honest with her, we really didn't want her to waste her time or money on greenery.

"Listen, Jane, you are incredibly thoughtful to want to help spice up the sanctuary, particularly since you won't even be there, but to be perfectly honest with you, it doesn't make a bit of difference to us if there are plants lining the aisles or not. Save your money and spend it in Hawaii, sister, no doubt you'll need it."

She was determined to bless us in some way. "Well, if you don't want plants, what *do* you want?"

"Not a thing, Jane except your prayers—just pray for us, we need it!" She was persistent. "Where are you going on your honeymoon?"

I explained that we weren't really going to have a honeymoon until we got back home from the tour. We had discussed maybe going down to New Orleans for a few days once we got back to Mississippi, but we would be on the bus with everybody else until we got home. Some of the dancers had joked us about the possibility of putting up some curtains on the bus so we could at least have a little privacy on the trip home.

"Well, where would you *like* to go on your honeymoon?" she asked.

I chuckled, then sarcastically asked, "So Jane, are you going to *buy* us a honeymoon to the destination of our choice?"

"No I'm not going to *buy* you a honeymoon," with equal sarcasm in her voice.

"But we can pray can't we? God can do anything! Where would you like to go if you could go anywhere—*anywhere*?"

"Gosh, I haven't really thought about it because there's no way we can afford a bona fide honeymoon trip. Let's see . . . I've got it! Deana and I would love to go to some exotic island, somewhere like the Virgin Islands, or the Bahamas, or Aruba! That would be awesome!"

I thanked her for loving us enough to call us and wanting to bless us on our wedding day, and we ended the conversation.

A few days later she called me back. When I answered the phone she identified herself, then asked me if I was sitting down. I still remember the excitement in her voice.

"Tim, you are not going to believe what I'm about to tell you. Mike and I were at a Dunkin Donuts in Harrisburg a few days ago enjoying a doughnut. We noticed a display on the counter encouraging patrons to drop their name and address in a box for a chance to win a free vacation trip. We put our name in the box. Tim, the people at Dunkin Donuts headquarters called a few hours ago and announced that *we had won the vacation trip!* We thought it was one of our friends playing a joke on us at first, then we remembered that we really had signed up. It turns out that ours was the name picked from all of the entries, but part of what we 'won' was an 'opportunity' to take a look at a condominium while we were there on vacation. They were hoping to sell us a time-share in a condo once they got us there. I've spent the last several hours on the phone asking them if this dream trip is transferrable. I explained that you and Deana are sort of like missionaries, and definitely could not afford to purchase a time-share in a condo, but if they would allow us to give the trip to you, that's what we want to do. I also explained to them that you guys would want to go in September. Tim, they said we can do it! *The trip is yours!*"

I was completely dumfounded. I simply could *not* believe my ears. Was I dreaming, or did I just hear from a reliable source that Deana and I were going to be able to go on an *all-expense paid honeymoon trip*?!

Guess what? We *did* go and it was incredibly wonderful! But do you know what is infinitely more incredible? The unending love of God put on display by blessing us with such a trip. His attention to the details of our lives absolutely boggles the mind! His creative genius is limitless! God caused a man and his wife in Pennsylvania to have a sudden urge for a dessert, *but not just any dessert*. They specifically wanted to eat a *doughnut*. They could have gone for a soft pretzel, or an ice cream cone, or a piece of pie at some other restaurant, but *no!* God caused their taste buds to tell them to go for a doughnut. They could have gotten a Krispy Kreme doughnut, but they went to a Dunkin Donuts store—and one that happened to be participating in this vacation giveaway program.

And finally, the hand that reached blindly into that box full of slips of paper *just happened* to grab the *one piece* that had the Prestosh address written on it. Our loving God chose to give a ballerina from Pennsylvania and a Bubba from Mississippi a free honeymoon.

The Master Artist had again painted a phenomenal set of circumstances on the easel of life. Unbelievably, the honeymoon package was a trip to the Bahamas! The Dunkin Donuts folks had decided a long time ago where the "lucky" winners of the vacation would go on their trip. Their company decided months before Jane ever called me to talk to me about our wedding. But we know it wasn't really the Dunkin

Donuts people's decision after all. It was in fact the Creator of creativity who had chosen the destination; and knowing Him, He probably made the decision sometime before you or me or Deana were even born.

9

Triplets? Are You Kidding Me?

A T THE CONCLUSION OF A Ballet Magnificat program in Bradenton, Florida, at a place called "Christian Retreat", John Vandervelde encouraged members of the audience to come forward with their prayer needs and allowed the dancers and me to pray for them. John was standing there perspiring all over the microphone, wearing this bright red, sequined, blouse-like costume thing (that's the technical name) that I would never wear unless God audibly commanded me to do so.

I can remember John encouraging the people to be askers, and seekers, and knockers, and to come down and let us pray for them. Many did come forward for prayer, but none more interesting than one particluar man who approached John.

He was an articulate, handsome man in his mid-fifties. He asked that John pray for his son and daughter-in-law who had been trying to have a baby for over a decade. They had been trying to get pregnant for 12 years but to no avail. They had been prayed for by countless people, countless times, but this parent was *still* standing in the gap for them. John prayed fervently that God would bless the couple by enabling her to get pregnant.

Fast forward about 18 months later, and we were in Indianapolis, Indiana, for a week-long "party" held annually in the Hoosier Dome. It is organized by singer-songwriter and Christian music icon Bill Gaither, and approximately 11,000 folks are in attendance each evening to enjoy a wide variety of Christian artists.

Ballet Magnificat was given booth space to sell our t-shirts, sweatshirts, videos, and distribute information about our school and touring ministry. The gentleman for whom John had prayed in Bradenton approached our booth and spoke to John.

"Hello John!" smiling broadly, he reached out for a hand shake. "Do you remember me?"

With an equally big smile, John warmly shook his hand and said matter-of-factly, "No."

They both laughed as the man realized John had met thousands of people since that night in Bradenton almost two years earlier. After reminding John about that night, and his prayer request, he clearly remembered the situation.

The man excitedly continued. "Guess what? My daughter-in-law is pregnant . . . *with triplets!*" The two men hugged each other in celebration. The man went on to say that people keep asking their family if she took fertility drugs, and they keep telling them that she did not, but that the Lord miraculously enabled her to conceive.

This was obviously a tremendous encouragement to all of the members of Ballet Magnificat. When things like that happen, and any of us have a role in the drama, it makes all the miles we travel, the set-ups, the tear-downs, and all the other grueling work seem eternally worthwhile. But there's more to this story.

The most amazing thing to me about the story is the faith displayed by the man who came forward for prayer that night in Bradenton. For *any* middle-aged man to humble himself to walk down an aisle in front of hundreds of people and approach a sweaty, male, ballet dancer with a prayer request is amazing to me. But this was not just *any* middle-aged man.

He was a practicing OB/GYN doctor. He had seen with his own, well-trained eyes why she should never, *ever* be able to conceive. His 30 years of experience had many times shouted at him, "It will never happen—you've seen for yourself! It's physiologically impossible!" He had explained to John that his daughter-in-law had endometriosis and a severely scarred, seemingly dysfunctional uterus. Fertilized eggs could not lodge because of all the scarring.

So the doctor knew far better than most people why—for all practical purposes—she would never conceive. He likened it to a car not having an engine and praying that it would somehow crank. He chose to trust the Architect who designed the human body, the Creator of medical science, rather than its "proven" principles. And he kept asking on their behalf. And the Creator granted his request. The parents are thankful for the doctor's stubborn faith. And they are wildly thankful to God for performing the miracle. One day the triplets will be too.

Boxer Baby

TRAVELING WITH A CHILD throughout this country can be extremely rewarding. It can also be extremely trying. The touring members of Ballet Magnificat stay in patron's homes more often than in hotels. On one occasion we were traveling through Texas and arrived at our host home about midnight, after having been on the road in the tour bus for almost 11 hours with no functioning air conditioner. Deana (my wife at this time) and I had not even met the gracious folks who would be hosting us, and our two-year-old son was crying uncontrollably. This is more than the normal I-wanna-eat-right-this-second baby cry. Think blood-curdling, doing pediatric surgery with no anesthetic type yelping. Anyway, as I reached to shake the gentleman's hand, the entire contents of our diaper bag spilled onto his front porch.

Not to worry. Thank the Lord the *only* thing that landed on his brand-new pair of Hush Puppies was a dirty diaper which was only slightly oozing from all sides. With the reflexes of a sedated box turtle, I lunged for the bag before it hit the porch, but in so doing, I knocked my wife's 400-pound suitcase directly into the man's shins. He grimaced and doubled over in pain, but quickly composed himself, straightened up, and smiled a nervous smile. It was one of those smiles you wear when you are unbelievably embarrassed or trying your best to hide the uncontrollable anger. He assured us over my son's piercing screams that he was perfectly alright.

We were getting off to a great start.

As we walked down the hall waiting for him to show us our room, he asked that we not let our luggage hit against the walls or let our child play unattended. Then he said he wanted to show us where we could put our "rubbish". I had never heard anyone, except perhaps in a foreign flick, use the word *rubbish*. Nor have I ever been instructed by a host as to *where* I should dispose of my rubbish. I just about always dispose of rubbish in garbage cans, but I figured I could make an exception for him this one time. Needless to say, we didn't exactly feel right at home at that moment.

The next day he and his wife were both at work so we had the house to ourselves. Around noon our son was ready for a nap, and we decided to take one too. We set up his pop-up crib in our hosts' master bedroom rather than in our room, because we were afraid the slightest noise would wake him. Everything was going swimmingly until about an hour later we heard little Mathias crying and so we went to check on him. I'll never forget what I saw when I walked into that master bedroom.

Mathias was standing up in his pop-up crib looking very proud of himself. At his feet were 19 pairs of the man's underwear. Oh yeah, I counted. In fact, he was wearing one pair on his head—the elastic was around his forehead so that it looked like a chef's hat. We had apparently put him within reach of the man's chest of drawers, and he had decided to empty it almost entirely. I began frantically gathering up all 19 pairs and folding them up. Crisis averted, right? Not so fast.

When I looked into this man's drawer, fear struck again. His underwear was *perfectly* folded, starched, and neatly arranged in a tidy row, military-inspection ready. And to make matters worse, each pair was monogrammed on the left thigh, facing up. *How on earth am I gonna replicate that?* I tried my best, but it was like folding a map—if you don't start just right, you won't end up just right.

Just when I thought things couldn't get any worse, it hit me. Deana and I would be leaving to go to the theatre long before he would get home. If I didn't fold them back correctly, later that evening he would get ready to attend the ballet, and discover that his "artsy guests" had plundered his underwear drawer.

Well, he and his wife *did* notice, and they *did* think the worst, but we were able to explain everything the next morning before we left town. It was not a good place for us to make a mess of things, although I suspect the Lord used it in the man's life to humble him just a smidge. I assured him that for him and his wife to think for a second that we would go through his dresser inappropriately was, well, *rubbish*.

Nobody Loves Me Busept Jesus

NOBODY LOVES ME busept Jesus." There was hopelessness and heartache in the voice of our three-year-old son Mathias. He really wanted a piece of fudge. But we really wanted him to get sleepy and go to bed.

He had asked me first and had gotten a firm "no." Then Deana had flatly refused his rebound request. This came as a major shock to his system because he's accustomed to Deana saying yes to requests like, "Mama, may I please fly to the moon this afternoon with forty-six of my friends, then treat all of them to McDonald's Happy Meals before bringing them over to camp out in our back yard?" So being denied the simple request for a piece of fudge was a jaw-dropper.

He repeated himself in an extremely whiny voice. "Nobody loves me busept Jesus."

His mother corrected him. "Nobody loves you *except* Jesus, Mathias."

He whipped around in disbelief. With tear-filled eyes and a broken heart, he cried out: "*You* don't love me either?!"

From Engineer to Balledude

"IS IT TRUE THAT YOU'RE gonna be a *belly dancer?*" he asked with a beleaguered look on his face.

This colleague, sitting in his cozy engineering office, could not believe that John Vandervelde would even consider such a bizarre notion. All these years John seemed so . . . normal. He wondered what caused him to lose his mind.

Of course, he was not considering becoming a *belly* dancer but a *ballet* dancer. His co-workers would be quite relieved—somewhat. But what in the world would cause a perfectly sane family man to give up what he had worked so hard to achieve?

Excelling in math and physics in high school had led John to the reasonable decision to pursue an engineering degree. He stayed the course and accomplished his goal. John graduated from the University of Alberta with a degree in mechanical engineering. He then married his high-school sweetheart, Karin, and set up residence in his hometown of Edmonton, Alberta, Canada.

It turns out that his father-in-law, a Danish immigrant, was president of one of the largest engineering consulting firms in Canada.

John secured a position in this firm. His course was well marked out for him; there was nowhere to go but up the corporate ladder.

So *what in the world* caused him to choose a different course? Nothing and nobody *in this world* did. Or could have. An out-of-this-world Choreographer had hand-picked John many years earlier for a specific role. There were thousands of more accomplished male ballet dancers. And most of them were not married. Most of them were not parents. Very few of them held college degrees. Most of them did not live in a nice home in the suburbs with a two-car garage and a fenced-in backyard. But this one was different.

During his time as an engineer, John decided to take a jazz class one night a week "just for fun". One night a ballet instructor introduced himself and encouraged him to consider taking a ballet class sometime. John was not interested in ballet *at all*. However, over the weeks the man persisted and John hesitantly agreed to take one ballet class. To his surprise, he really enjoyed it. It was considerably more challenging than he had anticipated, both mentally and physically. "Just for fun," he took another class. And then another. One night after class the instructor said something to John that was almost laughable.

"If you take this seriously, and continue to work really hard, you could become a professional ballet dancer in about a year or so."

John was both confused and amused. "Are you serious? How can you say that?" John asked.

The instructor explained to John that he had an exceptionally good physique for ballet, and that at the rate he was improving, he would most likely be strong enough to dance on stage in a year's time.

On his way home that night, John found himself thinking about this man's ridiculous proposal. *Why on earth would I want to become a ballet dancer?* he thought. "What would my wife and kids think? What would our parents think? My friends would think I had gone mad. Wait a minute, it doesn't matter what *any* of them would think, because there's absolutely zero chance that I'm going to pursue this ballet thing," he reasoned aloud to himself.

Later that night he told his wife Karin what had transpired earlier in the evening. He knew what her reaction would be; he just hoped she wouldn't wake the kids up with her laughter. He was dead wrong.

"You know John, I think it's the Lord's will," she calmly asserted. "Let's go for it!"

John was astounded. *Go for it?! Go for what?* he thought. *Just drop my mechanical engineering career and begin pursuing a career in the arts? Put my suits, ties, and briefcase in storage, and run down to the nearest dance outlet and buy a dance belt and some ballet slippers?*

Not only is the notion downright absurd, but even if it weren't, it would mess up all of their plans.

He and Karin had recently purchased 20 acres on a hillside in Alberta which was to be the picturesque setting for their dream home. They had carefully drawn the house plans which had an international flair (they are very well traveled). They had already enjoyed three trips abroad during his career as an engineer and planned for many more to come. The concrete foundation for their house was laid in the spring of 1981. And guess what? It's still there today. That slab of concrete is still there today, and there's no house on it. Why? Because God's plans were different from John's, and John and Karin submitted to His plan for their lives, instead of their own. It's that simple.

The Vanderveldes believed they were being called to leave the familiar and secure world of mechanical engineering and enter the unstable world of dance. After John received his year of training he landed a position with the Spokane Ballet Company in Spokane, Washington. His salary would be about one-sixth of what it was as an engineer. Soon after that, he and Karin heard about a fledgling ballet company in the States, in Mississippi of all places. It didn't seem like a logical move at all, but they committed to pray about it.

Once again it was Karin who boldly exclaimed, "Honey, I think we should go for it!" Most mothers of three children would probably have come to a different, more logical conclusion. But they loaded up the truck and moved to Mississippi, Jackson that is, steaming grits, humidity galore.

You may be thinking that it just doesn't make logical sense—and you're right, it doesn't. Ask Pharaoh to logically explain hail falling from a cloudless sky. Ask one of the many witnesses who observed Lazarus walking out of his own tomb to explain it. How about what Noah went through? A lyric from a Garth Brooks song sums it up:

> "Old Noah took much ridicule for building his great ark, but after 40 days and 40 nights he was looking pretty smart."

Perhaps I'm over emphasizing the point, but often God's plans for our lives don't seem to make good sense to us. We're left scratching our heads in confusion—or worse still, disagreement.

Does the bare foundation on their home site represent John and Karin's shattered dreams? Absolutely not. Under different circumstances, maybe, but they are thankful they were chosen for this unique role. They trusted the Choreographer then. They trust him now. They know that, "His ways are higher than our ways."

Just Buy A New Toilet Door

WEREN'T THEY EXPECTING US? How were we to get in? We couldn't see too far beyond the ornate wrought iron gate from the beautifully landscaped hill that rose to meet the horizon just beyond it. The massive electronic gate was a formidable barricade— even for our Greyhound bus. So there we sat, wondering how long it would be before someone would discover us and let us in. We didn't know the entrance code and couldn't reach anyone by phone.

It had been a really long day already. We had boarded the bus at 8:00 a.m. in Spring Arbor, Michigan, and traveled the 105 miles to a high school auditorium in Fort Wayne, Indiana. We had unloaded all of the equipment and costumes from the bus and completed our standard set-up in about two hours. Following set-up we usually scatter to five or six host homes, but that night all of us were to stay in this one home. That is, if we could ever get past this seemingly impenetrable gate. Just as I was about to suggest that we drive to a pay phone (yes, no cell phones at the time) so I could call someone within the fortress, the gates began slowly opening. There was still no one in sight.

Our bus lumbered up the gorgeous winding entrance to a fairly large two-story home. As we began to disembark, we noticed two golf carts speeding toward us from behind the house. Hardly speaking to us, the drivers began to load our luggage onto the carts. Though it was great to have our luggage carried for us, it seemed a bit odd. I was preoccupied with sleeping arrangements for the evening. I muttered to one of the dancers that I knew I'd be sleeping on the floor that night because, "There's no way all twelve of us will have beds." Anytime there were not enough beds, I was usually the one on the floor, because dancers need beds more than non-dancers . . . at least that's what they always told me.

One of the men overheard me and smiled broadly. "Are you talking about having to sleep on the floor in *this* house?" he asked, motioning toward the pleasant two-story house in front of the bus, the one with bright-red geraniums in perfect little planters just under the dormers.

"Yes, sir," I replied. I was a little embarrassed that he had heard my complaint that I usually let the dancers have the beds, you know, because they're dancers.

He smiled again and said, "Sir, that's the *gardener's* house. Just follow us, please." The two golf carts continued past the gardener's house, around a little wooded area. As we rounded the corner, we all stopped for a moment, mouths agape. There before us was a mansion considerably larger than any I had ever seen in person, with the exception of the Biltmore mansion in Asheville, North Carolina. Beyond the 7,000-square-foot main house was the three-bedroom, two-bath guest house, complete with a tennis court and swimming pool! In addition to the breathtaking landscaping, there were deer on their estate. The whole scene was . . . how shall I say it? Impressive.

Keep in mind that we stay in all sorts of places, and most of them are very accommodating, some more comfortable than others.

Our hosts differ a great deal from night to night. We stay with wealthy people and poor people, auto mechanics and medical doctors, Christians and atheists, and people of various ethnic groups. So we are very accustomed to a variety of accommodations, but this place was absolutely mind-boggling. It was a much needed respite from the rigors of tour.

The day after the program, we were loading our luggage onto the bus in preparation to leave, and the hostess came out to see us off. We invited her to step in and take a look at our home away from home. Our bus looked very, uh, what's the word I'm looking for . . . oh yes, *gross*. It looked quite lived in—dance wear hanging over the seats, a paper plate on the floor with a piece of yesterday's pizza, blankets and pillows everywhere, and a very neatly twist-tied bag of trash that had not yet been thrown out. The look on her face was nothing short of amusing. She was trying really hard to mask how completely disgusted she was.

"This is really . . . nice," she proclaimed with zero sincerity. "Wow, you must spend a lot of time on this bus, huh?" You could tell she was trying not to come in actual contact with the seats for fear of some monstrous strain of bacteria overtaking her. She made her way through the length of the bus, passing the twelve bunks, our makeshift costume rack, the four-drawer filing cabinet we used for t-shirts we sell, to the most prized possession on this vehicle—the toilet.

"Oh, you've even got a toilet!" She was trying to sound impressed, but you could tell she was almost nauseated. She had that tell-tale I'm-about-to-throw-up expression on her face. I knew that expression well. It reminded me of the time I was seconds away from being sick at a Little League banquet. (Indulge me for just a minute).

I'll never forget the big lady who offered me that fatal fifth piece of fried chicken. She was trying to practice hospitality, God bless her, but the smell of the chicken combined with her pencil-thin mustache, caused me to make a run for it. I looked at that lady the same way the owner of the mansion was looking at us now.

"This door won't seem to stay shut," she said frustratingly, trying to close the toilet door repeatedly, but to no avail.

I explained that the door latch didn't work properly, so the guys guarded the door for the guys, and the girls likewise watched out for each other. She was appalled!

"Why on earth don't you just buy a *new* toilet door?!"

We explained that they don't just have rows of toilet doors for buses at your neighborhood Wal-Mart. And even if they did, they would cost more than $8.95, which is about all we could afford at the time. So the luxury of a new toilet door was, well, a luxury. A few minutes later she asked the same question, with the same inflection in her voice, about the broken driver's side rear-view mirror.

"Why don't you just get a new rear-view mirror?"

In retrospect, it was a comical exchange. Paupers trying to explain to a princess the difference between "needs" and "luxuries". You've only got $108 to your name. Your bus is almost on empty, and it takes 140 gallons of diesel to fill it. The last meal you had was eight hours ago at a Burger King in Detroit. We need diesel. We need food. We need a new door for our toilet. Hmmm. Decisions, decisions . . . what to do?

She prayed with us, hugged each of us, and sent us on our way. A couple of weeks later I was in the middle of a phone call about a potential booking at our home office in Mississippi. A co-worker, Jeff Bieber, burst into my "office" (a desk with two partitions) with a letter in his hand.

"Tim, you've got to read this letter!" he shouted excitedly.

I put one hand over the receiver and mouthed to him, "Shhh, I'm on the phone."

"Tim, you gotta read it right now, man!"

I had never seen Jeff this excited or any grown man squirm like that, especially an ex-Marine. So I put the caller on hold and read the brief letter. I could not believe my eyes. It was from the woman near Fort Wayne. She was thanking us for staying with her and for praying for her and her husband. She offered her home to us the next time we were in the area. And at the end of the letter, parenthetically at the very bottom, were these words: "I hope this money helps you get a new bus."

She had shown a video of Ballet Magnificat to her sister, who had not been able to attend the program. Then the two of them decided to send us $20,000—*each!* Forty thousand dollars! *Forty thousand dollars!* We could buy a *bunch* of new rear-view mirrors and toilet doors with forty thousand dollars! Neither of us had ever even seen that much money. We hugged each other and started jumping up and down in celebration. I nearly forgot that I had someone holding on the phone, and I'm sure they could only imagine what was going on at the other end of the line.

We immediately barged in on the dancers' rehearsal and told them the news. You've never seen such celebrating! We decided to circle up and pray right then that God would show us how to use the money. There had not been much love in the love offerings lately, and we had not been paid a time or two. Should we use $10,000 of it for our immediate needs? There were fourteen of us on staff at the time, so that would give all of us a $700 "bonus". Or should we spend every bit of it on a new bus? We also needed direction on whether to upgrade our current bus or try to get a different (newer) bus. After praying about the matter, it was our unanimous decision to use all of the funds to purchase a better bus.

We shopped Los Angeles, Dallas, and made a number of calls to Nashville, trying to find a Greyhound bus for $40,000. The very best buy for the money was a charter bus for sale in our hometown of Jackson. The only problem was that the seller wanted $51,000. When we told him we only had $40,000, he began the negotiating process. We assured him that we believed him that he was trying to give us a good deal, but we had no more money with which to bargain. He was a bit frustrated and accused us of playing "hardball". We continued to ask God to help us get that bus or another bus that would suit our needs.

About a week later "something" came over the man, as he explained it, and he made us a deal. Including tax and the license plate, he sold us the bus for $39,983—seventeen dollars *less* than the $40,000 given to us by the sisters in Indiana. The Artist had composed yet another magnificent masterpiece.

The Desert and Delilah

I WAS SKEPTICAL FROM THE very beginning. Nothing annoys me more than disingenuous televangelists claiming to heal people or know what people are thinking. My attitude is wisdom to an extent, but I can be downright cynical, and sometimes even hateful. Some of the dancers joked me about it. Traveling around the nation we were fed a constant diet of supposedly true testimonies about God's miraculous interventions into people's lives. While some of the other members of our touring group swallowed the stories "hook, line, and sinker," I was extremely doubtful most of the time.

The phrases that gave me the most trouble were, "God told me . . ." or, "Then the Lord said . . ." The testimonies would have been much more palatable to me had these people not used these phrases. Or at least they should have toned them down to the more acceptable, "I sensed in my spirit that the Lord . . ." Of course *my* opinion is perfect and *my* perspective on *everything* is also perfect, so why couldn't these folks "sense" this about me and tell their stories in more believable ways?

I'm certain at least one of the reasons I've experienced first-hand so many "curious" events is due to the harsh attitude I once had toward my more charismatic brothers and sisters. I've learned through the years that the Artist can do whatever he wants, however he wants to do it. So here are two stories I didn't volunteer to share during the ordination process for me to become a Presbyterian minister (uh oh, I hope this doesn't invalidate my ordination). Anyway, I've *sensed in my spirit* that the Lord would have me share two of these experiences with you, because maybe you, too, have been cynical at times. Here goes.

My hands were killing me! I had no idea why they were hurting so badly and even beginning to swell. I was driving our tour bus through a southwestern state en route to our next program and could hardly grip the steering wheel because the pain was too intense.

What on earth was the problem? By the time we arrived later that afternoon my fingers were so swollen I couldn't get my wedding band off. My hands were red and itchy and hurt deep down to the bones. Both hands were throbbing in sync with my heartbeat.

That night at our host home I told Deana that I thought it might be rheumatoid arthritis, because my Dad had the disease when he was a young man. I also told her that I was afraid. This made her afraid, because I didn't usually fret about little ailments. I told her that the pain was mostly in my right hand, but that my left hand was also hurting. I couldn't even grip the toothbrush to brush my teeth before going to bed. She prayed for me, and we dropped off to sleep.

The next morning we attended a worship service at the sponsoring church where we would be doing the program that evening. I was tremendously critical—sinfully critical—of the worship band. They sounded fine, but, well, they were *different*. You know, they didn't dress anything like I dress. And they didn't move around anything like I move around when I'm worshipping. Even their jewelry was really . . . ya know, different. And their hair was, well, you get the idea.

Suddenly my stream of critical and judgmental thoughts was interrupted. Their pastor and his wife joined the worship team on stage, and they were even more different. I thought ugly thoughts. I whispered critical comments to Deana. I was much too consumed with criticizing their every move to be able to worship. And then it got worse.

The pastor motioned for the band to stop playing for a moment. "The Lord says there's a spirit of healing in here this morning," he said.

I rolled my eyes so far back into my head I'm surprised they didn't get stuck and thought even more smug thoughts.

"Some of you need healing today," he continued.

My thought-life was vicious at this point. I remember thinking that *he* needed to be healed of his haircut, how he needed healing of that awful suit, how he . . . well, let's just leave it there. But I truly did believe he needed to be healed from his thinly veiled attempts at sincerity. He hummed a line from the song we had been singing while the crowd waited in anticipation for what would come next.

"There's someone here this morning who has been having a great deal of trouble with headaches lately," the pastor confidently asserted. "Be healed in Jesus' name!"

I rolled my eyes again. *That's an incredibly safe guess,* I thought cynically. I mean, come on, in a crowd of 400 people *somebody's* been having headaches lately. Give me a break.

"There's someone else who has had a nagging kidney infection. Lord, we pray that by Your power You would take away that infection."

I whispered to Deana, "I hope he stops this soon and gets on with this morning's teaching." God was no doubt becoming nauseated with my condescending attitude of cynicism and superiority.

The pastor then said, "The Lord says there's also someone here who's been having trouble with his hands. Lots of pain in your hands."

Okay, that was spooky. That one caught my attention. I felt the hair on the back of my neck stand on end. Deana squeezed my throbbing hand, and we both kept looking straight ahead, wide-eyed.

The pastor continued confidently. "Both hands have been in a lot of pain lately, particularly your right hand, but your left hand has been hurting you too. *The Lord says* for you to stop worrying about arthritis, don't be afraid, it's not arthritis, you'll be fine in a couple of days."

What is this? Am I on Candid Camera?

I couldn't believe my ears. Nobody in the world knew about the problem I was having with my hands except my wife and God! This man had even used the *exact* words I had used with Deana the night before in the bedroom in which we were sleeping! There is no way he could have discovered that information from anyone. No way, no how.

Never again would I "judge a book by its cover"! My hands did, in fact, heal over the course of the next few days and haven't bothered me since.

But just in case you were wondering what caused the reaction, it was my precious wife who finally figured out what had caused so much pain in my hands. She reminded me of something that had happened the day before.

I had gotten up early and decided to take a bike ride, because I had never ridden a bike in a desert, and it was an absolutely gorgeous morning. My host family let me borrow a bike, gave me a canteen of water, and pointed me in the direction of a bike trail in the desert. At one point I got off my bike to explore. I got down on my hands and knees and got my eye about two inches from a tiny blue desert flower—its brilliant color and the symmetry of the petals were magnificent! I was utterly mesmerized. No accidental or purposeless explosion could produce such beauty. Adios! "Big-Bang" theory, if you ask me. *Thought* went into the creation of something so beautiful. Artistic thought.

I then walked up to a large cactus, a saguaro, and studied it like someone in an art gallery would study a painting by van Gogh. It was spectacular. I was not only impressed with the integrity and strength of its protruding needles, but there were also these tiny, almost microscopic filaments covering the entire trunk of the cactus. They looked so soft, like eyelashes. I knew better than to touch the sharp needles, but I wanted to feel these little hair-like protrusions. I gently reached out to stroke the fuzzy little "hairs" and upon contact a bunch of them came off the cactus and clung to the index finger of my right hand. When blowing them off didn't work, I then took my left hand and started picking them off a few at a time. They were sticking *to* my fingers but not *in* my fingers and there was no pain at all—until I was driving the bus later that day. (No doubt you're ahead of me). Yes, I had cactus-poisoning in my hands. The pastor was absolutely right on target. I am convinced that it was not *merely* a coincidence.

Another seemingly inexplicable thing happened when Ballet Magnificat was at a church near the East Coast. We had finished setting up our equipment and had gathered to have our devotional time about two hours before the program was scheduled to begin. I was very tired on this particular afternoon and was less than enthusiastic about this pre-program worship time.

The dancers began singing some of their favorite songs. I'm embarrassed to admit I wasn't very "devoted" that afternoon and was just sort of lip-syncing. It was during this time that I "heard" loudly and clearly, "There's a spirit of Delilah in this place." I put the word "heard" in quotes because it was not an audible voice, but I'm positive that I clearly heard—or thought—that sentence.

It startled me and got my attention. I sat up straight in my chair and started singing along with the dancers. A few moments later I heard the same thing again—no more, no less. "There's a spirit of Delilah in this place." I had heard of a Jezebel spirit, but "a spirit of Delilah"? After our devotional time, I walked out to our bus, sat on the sofa, and read the story of Samson and Delilah. I was trying to figure out why I had "thought" or "heard" this same sentence twice. I closed the Bible and chalked it up to indigestion. No St. Augustine moment for me. I mean, it couldn't be God Almighty saying something directly to me—no way. Even if He did want to say something like that to someone, He would choose a less cynical vessel, right?

The program began and just before intermission the sentence was playing over and over in my head like a broken record. I considered going backstage to talk to my friend John Vandervelde about it, but he's one of the dancers and was currently in costume, and what could he tell me anyway? I told myself to just chill out. Besides, it was almost intermission, and I could talk to someone then.

About midway through the second half of the program I started hearing it, or thinking it, again. Just before the last song of the evening, I *finally* believed that it could be God speaking to me. (For all you non-Charismatics out there, just stick with me for another minute here). I run our lighting and sound equipment so I waited until the song had just begun, and then hurriedly walked across the aisles of people in the audience to where John was standing in the wing area. It would be time for him to run on to the stage in a matter of seconds, so I had to hurry. I nervously explained to him what had happened.

"John, all afternoon I kept hearing this sentence over and over, and then all through this program I keep hearing it. The sentence is, "There's a spirit of Delilah in this place." Maybe you should say something after

84

the program, you know, just before you dismiss the people. I mean, it could be from the Lord?"

John, drenched with perspiration, smiled at me very calmly. "It's definitely from the Lord, man, but *you* need to tell them."

"Me? No way! You know at the end, just before you dismiss them, just say that—"

"Tim, *you* have to tell them; the Lord spoke to *you*, and if it's for this group of people, *you* have to tell them. Sorry, man, I've got to go." And with that, he bounded onto the stage.

I hurried back to my post at the lighting and sound table. All of a sudden I was drenched with perspiration. My heart was pounding out of my chest. "Lord," I prayed, "help me out here. Do you want me to say something? They would look at me like I'm from Neptune. I don't want them to think I'm one of those looney guys on the television. And I don't know what *else* to say after I say the sentence about Delilah."

What does it mean anyway? How would it help anybody for me to go up to the microphone and say, "Uh, hello there. I've been hearing this random sentence for the last few hours and thought it would be good to share with you . . ." They'll just think "*Um, yeah—that's interesting . . .*"

The program ended. The audience gave a standing ovation. John walked over to the microphone and asked the folks to be seated. My heart started pounding even harder. Then he began his closing comments in his usual manner. I breathed a sigh of relief; my buddy knew better than to put me on the spot.

As he was finishing he said, "Brother Tim has something to share with you that he feels is from the Lord. Tim?" And he held the microphone out toward me. I knew God was compelling me to go forward, I just didn't have a clue why He would do such a thing. These people came to see ballet, not hear some guy from Moss Point,

Mississippi tell them something about a female in the Bible named Delilah! I made my way to the front, praying every step along the way something drastic would happen so I wouldn't have to get up there and make a fool of myself.

No such luck. I reached the front and John handed me the microphone. No doubt the people could see that I was nervous. The sweat dripping into my eyes and onto the dance floor gave them a pretty good hint. I hesitated for a moment. The silence was deafening. *Here goes.*

"I had hoped John would share this with you. We don't normally do this. I *never* do this. Anyway, uh, something happened this afternoon during our devotional time. I believe the Lord spoke to me and said, 'There's a spirit of Delilah in this place.' I don't know what it means. I read the story of Samson and Delilah, and I still don't know what it means. But I kept hearing that sentence over and over even during the program, 'There's a spirit of Delilah in this place.' I heard someone teach one time to never add to what the Lord impresses on your heart, so I'm not going to. Uh, well, that's all."

I handed the microphone back to John, just thankful I survived the moment.

I'll never forget what happened next. John invited people to come forward for prayer like he does after almost every program. Many people came forward to receive prayer. No surprise there. But a member from the church in which we had performed the program came up to me and excitedly said that what I had said was "definitely from God."

This person explained to me that there was a group of people in their church who wanted the senior pastor to step down from his position. They had been doing and saying things in an attempt to *take away his strength* as the leader of the church! (Delilah cut Samson's hair off to take away his strength). This person believed God used an outsider to confirm to everyone in their church that this had been going on. He also felt this would serve as a confirmation to the pastor (as well as a warning to those who had been trying to cut his strength) that he was in fact in God's will to be the senior pastor of their church.

Then, if that wasn't incredible enough, another woman came up to me with tears in her eyes and said, "What you shared was from the Lord, and it was for my husband! He's been the pastor of our church for over 30 years, and there are those who have been trying to get him to leave. They've been trying to strip him of his authority as pastor by making his every decision, no matter how insignificant, first go through the elders. We've been so confused, and we've even begun second-guessing ourselves, wondering if it is God's will that the authority he has should be cut from him."

I told her I'd like to pray with her about the situation. She agreed. Just before I prayed I asked her, "Does everybody here (I motioned around the room) know that this has been going on?"

"Excuse me?" She looked confused. "Why, nobody *here* knows what's been going on."

Now I was confused. She saw the confusion on my face and explained. "My husband and I are not from this church. He pastors the church *across the street*."

God had spoken directly into *two entirely different situations!* Members from two different congregations, whether well-meaning or not, were trying to undermine the strength of their respective pastors. There was probably not one person from either church who knew what was going on at the other church, but God knew exactly what was going on!

I was utterly amazed (and still am when I think about it). The Bible is absolutely, positively complete, and is God's perfectly sufficient, inerrant, and true word. But God encourages His children in many ways. The Lord had spoken that evening, and people knew he had spoken. I suspect some of the people in that room felt encouraged, even comforted. Others probably felt exposed, and maybe ashamed. I felt both encouraged and ashamed. I was encouraged that God stooped to minister to the specific situations and precious folks of those two churches. And ashamed that I almost let my prideful discomfort prevent me from speaking.

I learned two lessons from these experiences that I'll never ever forget. First, don't handle a saguaro cactus under any circumstances. Second, if God can speak through a donkey (Num. 22:28), or even worse, someone as cynical as me, then he can speak through anyone he chooses, any way he chooses, at any time he chooses.

Airbag Angel

FOLLOWING A PROGRAM in Pittsburgh, Pennsylvania, a man approached one of our male dancers, Michael Cadle, and asked if he could pray for Michael. Usually people from the audience come forward to meet with one of the dancers, and often ask the dancer to pray for them. But in this case, the man wanted to pray, and Michael relates that he began to pray a perfectly "normal" prayer for Michael and his wife Mary, who was also a dancer in the company at the time.

"Lord I pray you would continue to bless this man and his wife as they dance for your glory. I pray that you would keep them safe from injury while they dance, and as they travel around the country. I thank you for showing them how they can use this art form to glorify you, and I thank you so much for the airbag angel. Lord, I also pray that you would bless them financially and . . ."

He interrupted himself and asked Michael, "Did I just say 'airbag angel'?"

A bit confused himself, Michael confirmed that those were the words he used in his prayer. The man smiled, shrugged it off, and continued to pray.

About an hour later the bus was loaded and began the journey home to Jackson, Mississippi. Estimated driving time: approximately 17 hours. The next afternoon Michael just happened to be driving his shift as we were going through the state of Tennessee. Most of the dancers were asleep. Something caught his attention in the rearview mirror; flames were shooting out of the driver's side rear wheel! The bus could blow up at any moment!

Michael yelled for everybody to wake up as he was trying to determine whether to pull over and bail out immediately, or if he could make it to the top of the hill to a service station he could see. He decided on the latter, and the instant the bus stopped at the station, everybody bolted off the bus.

After extinguishing the fire, a mechanic called Michael over to show him something up under the bus. "You folks are mighty lucky," the mechanic began. "That there coal hot thing is your tag axle (it was still glowing orange like an ember), and that big square thing just above it is your gas tank. That thing that looks sorta like an oversized accordion separating the axle and the fuel tank is your airbag. I 'spect she would've blown sky high if it weren't for that there airbag."

Michael got goosebumps. He remembered that the man in Pittsburgh had explicitly thanked God "so much for the *airbag angel*"!

Logic Can Be Tragic

T HE ENGINE OF THE BUS had finally warmed up enough so that the heater was working, and the dancers were beginning to thaw out. It was a chilly February morning, and everybody was looking forward to heading toward balmy Southern California. We were fueled up and had loaded the costumes, dance flooring, lighting equipment, and sound system. The luggage had been carefully stowed away, and all of the dancers were sitting on the bus and ready to take off.

There was only one thing missing—money. (Minor detail). Including our personal money, we didn't even have enough for lunch and the next fuel stop, let alone a five-week tour that was to take us through several states en route to the west coast. It was so pitiful that it was almost funny. Seven professional ballet dancers and a bus driver/technician were sitting on a bus at 8:00 a.m. ready to go on tour, but with no money. We decided to pray. And then we prayed some more. And then we just sat there, trying not to feel too foolish.

We had been praying for several weeks for sufficient funds to be able to make the trip. There had been many hours spent in choreography and rehearsals, and we had even planned our route, knowing all the time that if God had opened doors, he would provide the way for us to do what he had called us to do. And we continued to sit in the parking lot. Nobody was "unspiritual" enough to suggest that we cancel the tour, but all of us were beginning to question God in the privacy of our hearts.

Almost an hour had passed when a familiar van rounded the corner and pulled alongside our bus. It was Kathy Thibodeaux's father, Bo Denton. He thought we had already left town, and he just "happened to be passing by". Needless to say, he was amazed when he found out why we were just sitting on an idling bus. He went to the bank and returned with $800, enough to get us to our first program and offering.

One might ask why we had even bothered to set our alarms the night before if we didn't have enough money for the trip. It wasn't because we were mighty men and women of faith *at all*. The Bible says in Hebrews 11:1, "Now faith is being sure of what we hope for, and certain of what we *do not see*" (emphasis added). The reason we all showed up that morning was because we *had seen* God provide time and again when we saw no realistic or feasible way. We had learned that sometimes it was best to keep moving ahead, even when it didn't necessarily make sense.

The apostle Peter had to get out of the boat *before* he knew if he could walk on water (Matt. 14:28-29). His faith preceded his action, but there *was* action. He did *do something* as a result of his faith. We shouldn't allow ourselves to become anesthetized to this oh-too-familiar story. Peter's intense faith, although short-lived, caused him to boldly approach Jesus, literally stepping out onto water. His faith literally affected the decision he made to do something seemingly ridiculous. Sometimes we just have to get out of the boat!

Can you imagine what Peter's friends were saying to him, and to each other?

"Hey goofy, what do you think you're doing? You're gonna sink like a rock!"

"I can appreciate Peter's faith, but he's taking this thing a bit too far."

"Doesn't he know that no one has ever done that before?"

"Poor thing, he just isn't very smart is he?"

"Some people will do anything to impress their boss."

Before we discard these hypothetical reactions as outlandish or comical, let's ponder for a moment what *our* reaction would have been had we been in the boat. I'm sorry to say that I probably would have murmured one of the above responses. In fact, I have said very similar things to folks who find themselves on the precipice of a cliff that will measure their faith. We should be the first to encourage people to step out in faith, rather than trying first to dilute their faith with logic. Logic, when separated from faith, can be tragic. If one's eyes are riveted on Jesus, as Peter's were when he asked his permission to come to him on the water, one can be sure God will be honored by his or her step of faith.

David didn't kill Goliath merely by staring at him, nor did he over-spiritualize the situation and decide to "just wait on the Lord". He didn't sit around playing the harp, praying that Goliath would have a heart attack and just drop dead. David, because of his unfaltering faith, decided to *do* something. Shouldn't he have prayed for a season? Shouldn't he have sought counsel? Maybe form a committee or something?

David was a worshipper and a *warrior*—not a *worrier*. Because he lived a *life* of prayer, there was no need for a *season* of prayer. He knew something of the character of his Lord, and he knew that God was not pleased with this "uncircumcised Philistine" taunting the army of the living God. So he took action. He bent down and selected five smooth stones for the task (1 Sam. 17:40).

God did the rest, but David did *something*. No doubt there are seasons in all of our lives in which waiting on the Lord is His will for us at the time. But there are clearly times when He wants us to go off the high dive blindfolded. He may even choose to keep us in the dark as to whether there is any water in the pool!

It's interesting to note that David selected five smooth stones. If he was really so full of faith, why didn't he pick up just one stone? Was he worried that he might miss? We can only speculate about this, but the important thing is that he *did something*. He put the remote control down, got up off the couch, and did something. Rather than join the others in a pity-party of cowering and whining, he did something. Instead of immersing himself in an ocean of logical reasoning, David took action to get rid of his ugly, giant foe. His weapons? A rinky-dink slingshot, and a childlike faith in God.

That same God, the one who enabled little David to slay Goliath, enabled us to drive on toward California with the certainty that he was going to meet all of our needs—and he did just that all along the way.

Neil's Bludgeoning

S OME OF THE FUNNIEST things in life aren't funny at all when they first happen. But at some point later on, it becomes a funny memory. Maybe a week. Maybe a year. Maybe longer.

We were performing a program in central California in a state-of-the-art high school auditorium. The set-up process had gone smoothly, the lunch provided to us was splendid, and everything had gone as planned. Everything was right on track.

About thirty minutes into the program, in the black-out between songs, we flooded the stage area with fog from a theatrical fog machine. We used box fans on both sides of the stage to get quicker coverage, because we don't like to keep the audience in total darkness more than a few seconds.

On this particular evening, we successfully achieved the desired effect, and the dancers were beautifully dancing in the fog. Suddenly, something like strobe lights flashed all over the room, and an extremely loud smoke alarm system screamed *NANK! NANK! NANK! NANK!* Some of the audience bolted for the exits, others looked at me for answers, still others seemed to think it was all part of the show. None of us were happy campers.

It was an ugly interruption to a beautiful and dramatic part of the program. The fog we purposely produced and floated onto the stage had set the alarm off. We had checked earlier in the day if this would be a problem and the school agreed to make the necessary adjustments to keep the fire alarm from enabling.

The dancing stopped. The music stopped. And by the time one of the dancers explained to the audience from the microphone what was happening, that everything was okay (and that nobody would die from a raging inferno), someone had shut off the alarm. The program resumed.

Sometime later, in *another* black-out between songs, there was apparently some kind of accident on stage. I heard a male voice shout loudly and unmistakably, "Guys, I'm hurt! Oh no, help! Guys, I'm really hurt, oh, ouch!"

It was our newest male dancer, Neil Berson, whose father had come this particular night to watch the program for the first time since Neil joined the company. He picked the wrong night.

Keith Thibodeaux was sitting with me where we had the sound mixer and lighting equipment set up in the very back of the auditorium. He realized it was Neil at the same time I did, and we both were aware that if we could hear him from the very back of the auditorium, then everyone in the audience could also hear what Keith and I quickly sized up as "melodrama". With the sensitivity of a third-world dictator, Keith looked at me and asked, "Do you want me to go back there and shut him up?!"

"*Please* go tell him to be quiet," I barked. "He doesn't realize how loud he's moaning. He probably stumped his toe." Keith bolted backstage.

I started the music for the next song, but when I brought the lights up the dancers still were not in their positions. Instead, my wife was walking around in front of the stage looking for the microphone. She picked it up and began explaining to everybody that there had been a pretty bad accident, and she asked them to please bear with us for a few minutes.

I cynically rolled my eyes, and headed backstage to see what she was referring to as "a pretty bad accident". I was slightly justified in my doubts, as I had seen Neil's reactions to other relatively minor injuries. But I was soon to be humbled, once again.

I hurriedly walked through the audience and across the stage to get to the dressing rooms. I could not believe my eyes. There were several *pools* of blood all over the stage. I hurried to where Neil was lying flat of his back, with a blood-soaked towel around his head, and one of the girls holding his hand. It looked like a scene out of *Gladiator* with blood splattered everywhere.

I noticed John's hand was covered in blood up to his wrist. John had been applying pressure to a large cut on the side of Neil's head. We learned later that in the black-out he had been accidentally putting pressure *right next* to the cut for the first few seconds, causing it to bleed even more profusely. I just wanted to know what was going on. "Will somebody tell me what in the world happened to Neil?"

They explained that Deana and Jirka Voborsky (a tremendously talented male dancer from the Czech Republic) had been moving the 90-pound wooden cross just behind the stage between songs like they always do. It slipped from their hands just as Neil was going by, and he collided with the cross.

Kathy and the others decided to quickly rearrange some of the choreography rather than cancelling the program. After a 20-minute "intermission", the ballet resumed while an ambulance took Neil to a local hospital for stitches. We finally finished the program, prayed with several people, and struck our equipment. We knew God must have wanted us to dance in that particular high school on that particular night, because it was quite evident the Enemy did not.

Bling, Rings, and Crazy Things

ONCE WE WERE THE guest entertainment for a monthly brunch given for the ladies of Harvest Christian Fellowship, a large church in Riverside, California, in the greater Los Angeles area. Most of the women in attendance seemed to be somewhat affluent, and they gave a standing ovation at the conclusion of the program. Immediately, I began to disassemble our equipment and take it out to the bus. Deana and I were engaged at the time, and she motioned for me to come meet a lady who was talking with her. I stopped what I was doing, and walked over to where the two of them were standing.

Deana said to the lady, "Tell Tim what you just told me." The lady proceeded to explain that from the time I had introduced Deana from the microphone to the audience at the beginning of the program, until the very end, she could hardly take her eyes off Deana's hands. Throughout the performance, she found herself continually trying to watch everybody on stage, but found herself focusing on Deana's hands. She didn't really know why, except that she had noticed that Deana was not wearing an engagement ring. The lady asked Deana if she had an engagement ring, and when Deana said no, she asked if she would like to have one. Deana smiled, and hesitantly told her that she would love to have an engagement ring, but that we had already discussed it and knew we couldn't afford to get one.

Then this curious woman who was much more modestly dressed than the other women, looked us both right in the eye and said, "The Lord is telling me to pray that someone would either give you the money to buy an engagement ring, or that someone would give you a ring." Then with an incredibly bold faith she continued, "I can promise you two things. First, I'm going to pray daily that God would provide an engagement ring for the two of you." (I must confess that at this point I was becoming very cynical in my heart, partly because I was in a hurry to take down the equipment, and partly because you meet a lot of interesting characters in Southern California). With penetrating eyes and a hint of a smile she continued, "Second, God *will* answer my prayers."

Two months later we did a program at a church called Cathedral of Praise in Oklahoma City, Oklahoma. As was our custom, after the program, we invited people to come forward to pray with one of the dancers if they felt so led. This particular night there were more people than usual asking for prayer.

About two months later, following a program at a church called Cathedral of Praise in Oklahoma City, we were meeting people who were patiently waiting in the queue.

The last two people in my line, a tall woman and a much shorter woman, were standing side by side so I assumed they were together. This was confirmed by the nature of what the tall woman wanted me to pray about. She confessed that during the dancing God had convicted her about a potential problem with adultery, and she began to share some intimate details. I wanted to ask her to pray with one of the female dancers (for propriety), but all of them were already praying with someone, and had more in line waiting. So I agreed with her in prayer, and she walked away. However, the other woman didn't leave with her. She just kept standing there with a glazed look on her face. I said, "I'm sorry, weren't you with her?" She did not respond to my question at all. I tried again. "Well, do you want me to pray for you?" Still no response. Then she silently held out one hand to me as though she were going to hand me something. I thought it was a note, or possibly some money that didn't make it to the offering. When I held my hand out, she dropped a golden ring into my hand.

Once again, I was dumbfounded (you'd think I learned by now, right?). "W-w-what is this?" I managed to stutter. "I mean, I know it's a ring but . . ."

She finally spoke. "Sir, I'm not a crazy lady—I'm really not. You can ask any of these people; I'm the pastor's secretary, and I just don't do stuff like this. It was the oddest thing. From the time you introduced your fiancée throughout the entire performance I could *not* stop staring at her hands. I noticed that she wasn't wearing an engagement ring, and I kept trying to watch everybody on stage, but I couldn't keep my eyes off her hands. Anyway, I'm not crazy, I'm really not, but I *know* that God wants me to give you two this ring. Would you use it as an engagement ring, or a wedding band?"

I was utterly stupefied. I told her that I suppose we would use it as a wedding band, since, technically, engagements rings are not a necessity but wedding rings are. And, I further reasoned that it didn't have any diamonds, and I've always thought of engagement rings as having a diamond.

"You know you're absolutely right," she replied, digging to the bottom of her purse. "Here's an earring with five small diamond chips in it. I bet a jeweler could set these in it for you. Then you could use it for whichever you wish.

The Master Jeweler, infinitely skilled at His craft, had provided a tangible and personal gift of love for Deana and me. He also increased our faith through the example of the prayer warrior back in California who had promised to pray.

One year later we did another program at Harvest Christian Fellowship, where we had done the brunch, except this time it was a church-wide event. About 1,500 people were there that night. During a costume change I told them the story from stage about the woman of faith at the brunch a year earlier, how she prayed and her prayers were answered. We were hoping that she would be in attendance and come forward so Deana and I could meet her again. At the end of the program another lady came forward, and without saying a word handed Deana *another* ring—a diamond solitaire that was a perfect match for her finger (it didn't even have to be sized!).

After that night, the dancers suggested that I start telling *bus* stories as well as ring stories.

19

"Little Ricky's" Pink Steak

"OH BUMMER, THEY COOKED this way too long," Keith Thibodeaux lamented. "Usually if I ask for medium-rare, they at least stop at medium, but look at this, it's well done, almost burned. I'm going to have to send it back."

Keith doesn't usually complain about much, especially for a Hollywood actor. None of us complained when a steak was in front of us. However, it really was *well* done. The main reason we stopped at this particular restaurant was to stay away from fast food. If this was going to be our one "good" meal of the day, and if we were going to spend good money for his steak, then it should be cooked at least somewhere in the neighborhood of medium-rare.

Now I wanted to complain. As usual, we were on an extremely tight schedule, and I knew that by the time he lassoed the waitress, delicately explained the problem, and got his replacement steak, we would lose at least 20 minutes, if not more. I can't remember if I complained out loud (probably did), but in my heart I was frustrated, even though I saw with my own eyes that it really was over-cooked. My agenda to arrive at our destination on time was much more important to me than how his steak was cooked. Which reminds me, my brother Mack, on the other hand, had a friend who liked his steak crazy rare. He would ask the waiter to "just knock his horns off and wipe his butt and bring it to the table." How charming.

It turned out that getting the steak right did cost us about thirty minutes before we were on our way. About twenty miles down the interstate, traffic came to a sudden halt, and we could see many, many police cars, fire trucks, ambulances, and other emergency vehicles, as well as one of the biggest wrecks we had ever seen. The east- and west-bound lanes were blocked with wrecked tractor trailer trucks, passenger cars, and other vehicles. I didn't count them, but there were probably fifteen or twenty *wrecked* vehicles, not counting all the emergency vehicles. There had been a horribly tragic chain reaction.

After one of the dancers prayed for all of the poor victims and their families, and we made it past the emergency area, almost an hour had passed. I got out the atlas to see how far we had come, so I could determine how much further behind schedule we were at that point. This would enable me to call ahead and let our sponsor know about the change in our projected arrival time. The atlas confirmed that we had made it twenty miles past the restaurant.

Then it hit me like a ton of bricks. The restaurant where we had eaten was right on the interstate, so it had taken us about twenty minutes to arrive at the scene of the accident. Assuming it took the emergency vehicles at least ten minutes to respond, that would mean that the wreck actually happened about thirty minutes earlier. Are you thinking what I'm thinking? Maybe not. What I'm thinking is that it took about 10 minutes for Keith to be served his medium rare steak, and if he had not sent his steak back, it would have been quite *possible* that we could have been in the wreck. Granted, we could have missed it by two or three minutes one way or the other, but the facts put us at the scene of the accident almost exactly when it took place if we had left that restaurant thirty minutes earlier.

Whether or not we would have actually been involved in the accident is not the point. The point is that our lives are fragile, we are in God's hands, and he is a loving and merciful God. We will never know how many times he has protected us, how many times our lives have been spared by his grace. Not by our intelligence. Not by our planning or savvy. But by his amazing grace.

And by the way, Keith said it was cooked perfectly the second time.

Stowaways

"OH NO! GUYS, COME look at this!" screamed Czech dancing sensation Petra Grusova. Although she's usually the quietest person on the bus, she continued to shout, "Look at this bag of snacks—and, *ugh*, look at this package of cookies! Oh, *sick!*"

I was driving the bus and didn't know what they were looking at, but I could tell by all the groans and moans that it had to be pretty disgusting. "There's a mouse on the bus!" said Kathy, "maybe even more than one." Those still in the bunks now bolted to the front of the bus, and they all examined the nauseating evidence. The bus doors had been left wide open at a 24-hour bus repair shop a couple of days earlier, and we were almost sure that was where we acquired the unwanted stowaways. There was no doubt about it, the package had been chewed open, and at this very moment we knew that we were sharing the bus with at least one furry little critter. At least we hoped it was only one. And little.

We were absolutely positive that it was on the bus with us, because we had been rolling since boarding that morning, immediately after being handed the "care package" of snacks and saying good-bye to our hosts.

What should we do now? Stop the bus and hunt for it? Keep rolling and hunt for it? Pretend there's no problem? Keith Thibodeaux took charge. "Bring all of the food on the bus up to the front, and when we get there we'll buy some mouse traps."

Over the next 48 hours the traps proved successful twice, making the dancers thoroughly sick but ending one more grotesque chapter in the history of our ministry. I wonder if the Joffrey Ballet dancers ever had mice on their bus. Probably not, they travel by plane.

See Ya Later, Alligator

W E DROVE THROUGH THE night from Charlotte, North Carolina, and had stopped for breakfast at a McDonald's just south of Memphis, Tennessee. As usual, some of the dancers chose to sleep through the stop, others went in for breakfast. It was a quick stop; everybody was ready to get the last three hours behind us and get home.

Three hours later, about one mile from our office, I announced that everybody needed to wake up and start getting their stuff together. Our dancers are a sight to behold after a strenuous program and drive through the night. No make-up on any of the girls, everybody's got severe bedhead, wrinkles across their tired faces, vastly different than the beautiful ballerinas on stage twelve hours—and 625 miles—earlier.

Suddenly, one of the dancers said Heather Faoila wasn't in her bunk. Another dancer responded through a yawn that she was in the restroom. The restroom door opened just then, and a sleepy *guy* walked out. Panic struck. Two or three groggy dancers hurriedly checked every bunk on the bus. Groggy and confused, we all just sat in silence for a moment. Then somebody exclaimed, "We left her at that McDonald's. We left Heather! We've got to go back and get her."

By now we were literally pulling into our studios, home sweet home in Jackson, Mississippi. We quickly called the restaurant to see if a slender girl in her early twenties had committed suicide there in the last few hours. They reported that a state patrol officer was driving her to Jackson, and she should be arriving about an hour after we did.

From then on, we all kept one eye on the bus when we disembarked anywhere.

And never you mind whose fault it was for leaving her behind. That's not important.

Thelma's Tornado

ONCE WE DID A PROGRAM in a small town in the great state of Georgia. I can't remember many details of our time there as vividly as I sometimes can, but I can well remember the frustration and anger I felt. I had been in contact with the lead pastor of the sponsoring church many times in the three or four months leading up to the program, and everything seemed to be in order; eight to ten men would be there when we first arrived to help us with the two-hour set up, the meals were planned, the host families secured, and active promotion was "bound to provide a packed house or close to it," which, according to the pastor, "will certainly provide even more than your $3,000 need."

An average "tour" consisted of two to three weeks on the road, performing ten to twelve times in three or four states. The various sponsors had a wide range of human and financial resources with which to work, resulting in a wide range of "success" in hosting the ballet. In other words, some were great, others, not so much. We prayed for strength and maturity to accept whatever was thrown at us, but certain times were more difficult than others.

This was one of those really difficult times. Maybe we were suffering more fatigue than usual, maybe the host church had not bathed it in prayer, maybe *we* had not bathed it in prayer, maybe (I can't remember) it was the third or fourth not-so-good-host in a row, it just seemed that everything about this program scheduled in the "Peach State" was discouraging. It wasn't that we were just imagining things. There was hardly any volunteer help available upon our arrival, the stage was much smaller than we had been told, and the volunteers who were there seemed downright annoyed that they were having to help us. Our host families evidently wanted the pastor to feed us at the auditorium before we came to their homes, and he came through with a fantastic meal of amazing grilled chicken, salad, and a variety of delicious vegetables. This was heartening, until we later discovered that he paid for it out of the offering given to us, which was considerably *less* than $1,000.

There were even more frustrating aspects of our stay, but you get the point. The dancers and I spiraled into a lower place than we usually did when things got tough, and we were discouraged regarding God's financial provision. Once we were together on the bus, heading to the next town, little hints of complaining began popping up. I'm sorry to admit that I didn't stop at just "little hints"—I openly grumbled and complained.

One of the dancers reminded all of us that "our light and momentary troubles are achieving for us an eternal glory that far outweighs them all" (2 Cor. 4:17). Someone else commented that thousands of missionaries through the years would love to have our "problems".

This prompted me to tell them about a friend of mine named Thelma, one of the toughest women I've ever known, and how her attitude toward suffering changed my life.

I'll never forget the look on sweet Thelma's face. This simple, uneducated woman was communicating volumes to me without saying a word. Her expression was telling of the incredibly difficult life she had quietly led, raising five young children through the heart of the Great Depression without the support of a mate. A dirt-poor black woman in the Deep South during the most trying times in American history—at least from a financial standpoint—and she survived.

What I saw when I looked into her huge brown eyes was love and character and wisdom. Wisdom borne not only from human experience, but time-tested and God-given *real* wisdom. She had experienced the grit and grime of eking out an existence in nearly unbearable conditions. If you asked her she would say the conditions would *definitely* have been unbearable, except for an all-important supernatural influence—God's grace. Miss Thelma was a living portrait of God's amazing grace.

And now she was being called on by this lily-white, college educated, white-collared, softy sales representative for consolation! Yes, I needed consolation, sympathy, and, oh, could you throw in some pity too, please, Miss Thelma? To what did I owe my pathetic and mournful state of mind? Just listen to this horrific, earth-shattering circumstance: I had not sold any equipment that month, so *I wouldn t be receiving any commissions*. Oh noooo! The world was no doubt just about to stop spinning on its axis! This was even more disastrous than the time I dropped the Cuisinart blender on my big toe just before my tennis match! Looking back on that day, I shudder to think what the mighty woman of God to whom I was whining must have been thinking. Knowing her, she was praying that she wouldn't fall into sin by judging me. What I deserved was a strong left jab planted squarely on my whiny little (chubby) face.

On numerous occasions, I had found myself shuffling into the dentist's office where Miss Thelma had labored for thirty-five years, hoping to be exhorted, edified, and/or rebuked (depending on the situation). Yes, at times I sought her out knowing she would rebuke me. Rebuking others is a very tough thing for most folks to do. But "tough" is a relative term. And Thelma certainly knew about *tough*. "Tough" is having to breast-feed all three of your youngest children to give them enough nourishment to survive. "Tough" is begging white people for their table scraps. It was "tough" for this illiterate woman to learn the alphabet at the age of thirty, then go on to teach herself how to type using only her two stubby index fingers. Suffice it to say that it didn't really stretch the limits of her endurance to occasionally set me straight.

The story she told me on this cold, damp morning knocked the spiritual wind right out of me.

"Mister Tim, I 'spect everythin's gonna be all right. I 'member one day back durin' de hard times (the Depression) I went to de kitchen to git de last can o' beans we had. I split it up 'tween my younguns de best I could. But de hardest part wuz watchin' their little faces look so confused, like I wuz greedy for eatin' so much of it. Dey didn't understand dat I had to eat some so's I could keep nursin' my three youngest ones. When we finished off dat last can o' beans, I just sat there for a minute. For de first time . . . I wuz scared. Mister Tim, I wuz *real* scared. I wished real bad I could git my chilluns out of dis mess. I didn't want them to starve to death, Mister Tim. 'Bout that time my littlest girl must've seen dat I wuz scared. She said, 'Come on mammy, let's go singin'!'"

She explained that often she would bundle up her children and take walks for fun. There was very little else to do for fun in those days. They didn't even have bicycles, much less a television or radio. She couldn't read to them, because she was illiterate, so there were very few books, and no children's books. All they had were a few homemade toys, a stray cat that survived off mice, and each other. That was it. Oh, yeah, and the Lord. They did have the Lord. Even the children knew that they had the Lord. And Miss Thelma had pounded it into their little hearts that nothing and nobody could ever, ever, *ever* take him from them no matter what happened. They often sang to him when they went walking.

The "littlest girl" probably had never been taught all the theological ramifications of worshiping, but she had, no doubt, enjoyed the smiles singing brought to her mammy's and brother's and sister's faces. Miss Thelma knew from experience that worshiping the Lord struck fear in the enemy, so she thought her daughter's idea was a good one.

"De devil could have all my fear. I didn't want it no ways. So I stuck my baby boy in de stroller Dr. Usher (the dentist she now worked for) had give us, and we took off walkin' and singin'. Directly, I'd forgotten 'bout our next meal and wuz singin' to de King."

It was at this point that I stopped fretting about this great woman seeing tears in my eyes, and I just let them go. She ignored the fact that I was crying, and kept ministering to me.

"You'll never guess what happened next, Mister Tim. You ever seen dem little baby tornadoes that throw leaves and stuff in the air only bout yea high?" she motioned with her hand.

I nodded yes.

"Well, my chilluns just luv to race to dem little tornadoes and bust 'em up by runnin' through 'em."

She paused and looked down at the floor. When her eyes met mine again, she was smiling a beautiful toothy smile, and now huge tears were rolling down *her* cheeks as well.

"One of my younguns picked up somethin' out of de leaves. He ran over to me to show me what it wuz. Mister Tim, it wuz a twenty-dollar bill! *Twenty dollars!* I could buy 'nuff food for me and de chilluns for *three months* with twenty dollars! I later heard folks say what a shame it wuz dat somebody lost dat money, tho' it wuz a blessin' that I found it. I don't believe nobody lost that money, Mister Tim . . . do you?"

Before I could answer she continued. "I tell you what I believe. I believe de first human hands dat ever touched that twenty-dollar bill wuz my little boy's. There ain't no doubt in my mind dat my *God* dropped that money on de ground just for us. He knowed what we needed then. He knows what you need now, Mister Tim."

Boy, was she ever right on target—you know, saying that God knows exactly what I need. As for the money never touching human hands until that day . . . well, I don't know. Knowing the infinite skill and bountiful mercy of the Artist, and knowing Miss Thelma, she just might be right.

Doc's Miraculous Oatmeal Decision

IT SEEMED TO BE ABSOLUTELY perfect for us! We had been checking the newspaper ads daily for a house to rent in the same vicinity as our office for $400 or less and found something that suited us. This particular house was less than a half-mile from our office, had a big back yard that our son Mathias would enjoy, hardwood floors, and the price was just right. We had been praying diligently that we would find the right house and neighborhood that would be best for our situation.

Our situation was that we had very little money. *Very little.* We were currently living in the house I had built before joining the ministry. I was a pharmaceutical sales representative for seven years prior to God calling me to Ballet Magnificat and during that time had built a nice home in a suburb of Jackson. The house note was about $800; no problem for a pharmaceutical representative. However, my financial status had changed dramatically when I joined the dance company. My "salary" with the ballet was approximately one-seventh of my pharmaceutical salary and considerably less than the $800 monthly mortgage payment alone. I put "salary" in quotes because back then, as mentioned previously in case you forgot, receiving our salary was often dependent on how much "love" was in the "love offerings" at each of our programs.

On more than one occasion, we had to take less salary than our need to ensure that the ministry had enough to meet its financial obligations. Ballet Magnificat was graciously supplementing our mortgage payment until we could sell the house and move into a more affordable rent house.

I had been trying to sell the house for over two years when it finally sold. This was great news, except for one problem. Deana and I had not yet found a place to rent. But we were sure we had struck pay dirt with this little house with the hardwood floors. I dialed the number thinking it was basically a done deal. Boy, was I wrong.

"Hello. My name is Tim Dry—"

A somewhat frustrated and monotonic voice cut me off. "If you're calling about the house, we've already rented it. Thanks for calling, good-bye." It sounded like a recorded message.

"No! Wait, wait just a minute please. Is there any way my wife and I could see the place on the inside?" I was desperately trying to keep a verbal foot in the door.

"Sir, I said it's already been rented. Thanks for calling. Good—"

"Ma'am, I'm sorry, I know you've already rented it, but it would really help me and my pregnant wife if we could get some idea of what kind of place we can get in this area for $400." Granted, throwing in the word "pregnant" was sort of a desperate tactic, but I needed to get her attention. I realize that I should have been trusting in God's power and not my throwing in a word like "pregnant", but I believe he gave me the idea to use it. And it was true for goodness sake.

"Well . . . I guess that will be all right. My husband has to stop by the house today after work anyway, and you could walk through it. But he's going to be in a hurry; he always is. If he lets you in, you better not dilly-dally. And remember, it's already been rented."

I thanked her profusely and assured her that I understood.

Her husband drove up exactly when she had said he would. He hurriedly got out of his new bright yellow Cadillac and headed briskly for the back door. When he rushed past Deana and me, he hardly acknowledged our presence. As soon as he got the door unlocked, he swung it open and said impatiently, "Well, here it is. Y'all can take a look around, but I'm only going to be here a minute. There's a rental application on the kitchen counter you can fill out and mail to us; we'll be glad to keep it on file. My wife told you it's already been rented, right?"

"Yes, sir," I assured him.

He was, in fact, ready to go in about two minutes. "I have to go now, but you can take your time, just pull the door to when you leave. It's already locked."

I followed him out the door, hoping to establish some kind of rapport. "Sir, my wife and I are in full-time ministry and our office is just around the corner on North State Street. Have you ever heard of Kathy Thibodeaux?"

"Kathy who?" he asked as he got in his car and started to shut the door.

"Kathy Thibodeaux, you know, she's the one that won a silver medal in world—"

"It was really nice to meet you folks, good luck finding a place," he said unconvincingly as he shut the car door and sped away.

I went back into the little house. Deana had the I-wish-we–could-have-this smile on her face. And, oh, how I desperately wanted to get it for *her*. My heart ached. "You really like it, don't you, sweet pea?" I asked optimistically, hoping my tone would help cheer her up.

She had a curious look on her face as she looked around the room. "It just seems . . . sorta like . . . like it's *already* ours or something. I mean it *feels* like home . . . doesn't it? Does it feel like that to you, too, like home?"

I told her that I knew exactly what she meant. It seemed more familiar to us than was normal for having only been in the place for ten minutes. Faith suddenly welled up within me. And joy. And boldness. I took Deana into my arms and told her that I felt very strongly that God was going to work it out so that we could rent the house. It was the kind of bold statement that a husband would normally only say to his wife, you know, in case it didn't turn out that way at all. (Okay, warning, warning. This is gonna get a little embarrassing, but it's true). We then faced each other, took each other's hands, and . . . danced; yes, *danced* around the living room and sang thanks to the Lord that he was going to give us the house. Deana wasn't accustomed to seeing me dance, although she was quite accustomed to seeing me do unusual things (which, I suppose might be one and the same).

She asked me if I really thought we might be able to live there because she honestly felt that it was a possibility. I told her that I believed it would definitely happen. We made sure the door was locked and left the house. We prayed about it and talked more about it that night, and our confidence grew that somehow God was going to provide the little house for us. I was hesitant to call the landlord again, but decided I would call the next morning.

His wife answered the phone. "Hello?"

"Hello, ma'am, this is Tim Dryden. My wife and I are the ones who called yesterday and asked if we could see your house, even though it has already been rented. Thanks for letting us do that. The house is great. I was just calling to tell you that if anything happens with the person you're planning on renting it to, please give us a call."

"Son, I doubt very seriously if that's going to happen. You see, we've already rented it to a single man who's moving here from out of town to work with one of our local television stations. He's already paid us a deposit, and it has cleared the bank. He seems rock solid, if you know what I mean. And even if something *were* to happen with him, there's a young married couple moving here from my husband's home town. They really want it, too, and my husband has known one of their parents for years. And, there's a third potential renter, should both of those fall through. I'm sorry, son."

"Oh, that's quite all right, I understand. Thank you, ma'am." We hung up. I was either very stubborn or had lots of faith. I'd like to think that Deana and I both had a stubborn faith. I was beginning to feel a little bit like Wile E. Coyote, never giving up on the Roadrunner, but I decided to write the landlord a letter.

Following is an exact reprint of that letter:

September 12, 1991
Dr. and Ms. Allen,

Thank you so much for calling me back and letting my wife and I look through your house and fill out an application.

We believe very strongly that it's the Lord's will that we move into that specific house. We prayed this morning about 8:00 a.m. that He would provide a place for us to rent for $400 or less within one mile from our office.

Your house was very, very clean, which made both of us very, very happy. It is exactly what we've been praying for, and if for some reason the other candidates do not work out, we would love to rent from you. I can assure you that we would keep the house and yard clean, pay in full and on time, and make you and the neighbors thankful that you rented to us. I do hereby agree to mow the yard whenever you deem necessary (with my mower and gas) and to your approval as part of the rental agreement.

I would welcome either or both of you to look through my home in Madison (in Tidewater sub-division)—I could tell you where there's a hideaway key.

Thank you again for letting us look through it, and please call or come by if it becomes available. We're in the Northwood Shopping Center, next to Shoetown. Work number: 982-3658 or 982-2144; Home: 856-8209.

Sincerely,
Tim, Deana, and Baby Dryden

Two days later Mrs. Allen called me at the office. "Hello, Mr. Dryden? This is Dr. Allen's wife. This morning my husband was reading the paper as he was having his oatmeal. Out of the blue he paused, looked up at me, and said, 'Honey, I think I'm going to rent the house to the little ballet couple.' He paused for a second, like he was about to change his mind, then he started eating his oatmeal again. I was shocked, to be perfectly honest with you. I mean, the T.V. guy didn't work out, but my husband didn't even ask me to call the young couple from his hometown or the other guy. It doesn't really make sense. I don't know why he didn't just go down the list like he usually does. Anyway, you can move in as soon as you pay the deposit."

That night during dinner I held my hand out toward Deana and told her that I had a surprise for her. She and I both love surprises. When she held out her hand, I dropped the keys to the little house into her hand. She was elated! When I told her what had transpired, she thanked the Lord.

The Artist had completed yet another beautiful piece of work. He had us smiling and shaking our heads in near disbelief. Wouldn't *anyone*—even someone who does not call himself a Christian—think something was odd about Dr. Allen saying what he said, as his wife put it, "out of the blue"? And wouldn't it also seem odd to *anybody* that he didn't "just go down the list like he usually does"? Deana and I know exactly why Dr. Allen acted out of the ordinary—because an extraordinary and loving Artist works twenty-four hours a day, seven days a week choreographing life's dance, right down to the most minute detail.

I am here reminded of that wise ancient saying, "The king's heart is in the hand of the Lord; He directs it like a watercourse wherever He pleases" (Prov. 21:1).

That verse also applies to the hearts of landlords.

Bottomed Out

A T THE END OF A PROGRAM in Loveland, Colorado, a woman approached me for prayer. I was standing alongside the dancers, where a crowd of people were coming forward to say hello, meet with their favorite dancer, or ask for prayer. It was obvious that the woman who was approaching me had been moved deeply during the program, tears had caused her mascara to trickle down her face.

"Do you people ever lay hands on those in need of prayer?" I could tell she was really hoping that my answer would be a resounding yes.

"We surely do. How can I pray for you?"

"Oh, thank the Lord." After a big sigh of relief, she continued. "I've been having excruciating pain in my hips for the last few days." She grimaced in pain, as she began rubbing her backside with both hands. "I think it's a pinched nerve or something."

Uh oh. What she thought of as "hips" appeared more to me like "buttocks". This could get really awkward.

At this point, she turned around with her back toward me. Apparently, she was ready for me to lay hands on her "hips" and pray for her! I was *not* ready to lay hands on her "hips" and pray for her. A bead of sweat developed on my brow. I glanced around for a female dancer to help me pray for this woman, but all of them were bowed, with their eyes closed, praying with people.

"Uh, ma'am, you can just turn around and face me, and I'll lay hands on your shoulders—God will hear just as well."

Crisis averted! Communication gaffes can be really funny in certain situations. The lady was thinking that I would lay my hands on her and pray for her—because I had just said I would—but we weren't on the same page regarding where exactly my hands would be placed.

CRISS-CROSSING THE nation for 12 years in a bus was very rewarding at many levels, but could be frustrating at times. We got lost on many occasions, sometimes because whoever was driving took a wrong turn, and other times because we were given faulty directions. Successful communication can be very elusive when a local is trying to direct us to our desired destination. And it seemed as though the later we were running on our schedule, the more likely we were to be given inaccurate directions.

I knew I was in trouble, for example, when I asked a local policeman for directions to a local college auditorium instantly looked confused, paused for several seconds, then stared off into the distance. "Okay. Here's what you do. Go straight up that way (pointing) for 2 or 3 miles, maybe 4, heck I don't know maybe 5 or 6, anyway, then make a right (but motioning *left* with his hand) on Bobwhite Lane. Keep going past where the old post office *used to be*, and in about a mile you'll see the Wal-Mart there on the right. You think you got it?"

"Well yes sir, but just a couple of clarifying questions. You said to make a right on Bobwhite Lane, but you motioned to the left. Did you mean to say go *left* on Bobwhite Lane?" I asked.

"Sure. You can turn left and still get there. If you want to turn left, then you'll need to—"

I interrupted. "No—no! I'll go ahead and turn right and go past where the post office used to be, but then you stopped when you got me to Wal-Mart."

"That's right. You turn at the four-way stop at Wal-Mart, and you'll see the college auditorium in about three minutes." I figured I'd rather keep my eyes open for a sign advertising the college, or even try all four directions than risk asking him the pesky little detail as to which way I should turn at the four-way.

ALTHOUGH I WAS delighted each and every time someone used a place that no longer existed as a landmark to help me on my way, that's not my favorite breakdown in communication. The one I like the most is when they hit me with that most genius question. It would surprise you how often the conversation goes something like this.

"Excuse me sir, may I please ask you a question about directions? I'm not familiar with this area."

"Sure. Where you headed?"

"We're trying to get to Cumbest Auditorium, and were told to take this exit, but we're not seeing what they said we would see."

"Oh yeah, they shouldn't have directed you to take this exit. I know exactly where that auditorium is. Let's see, *do you want the shortest route?*"

I usually just respond with, "Sure, that'd be great." But I'm always tempted to be rude with something like, "As opposed to what? The *next* shortest route? The longest route? The most convoluted, ridiculous, confusing, inaccurate route—what? Yes sir, I'd like you to give me the shortest—no wait. Take me through Omaha. I hear it's lovely this time of year."

I'M REMINDED OF another time when miscommunication almost cost me my life—well, *ahem*, at least a spanking.

On my eighth birthday my family took me tent camping where I could finally use my brand new flashlight. This one was the real deal. Had I been offered a motorcycle, a pony, ownership of the Atlanta Braves, or a flashlight, I would have opted for the flashlight. I cannot stress this point enough—I was *so* excited!

I regularly played with it in broad daylight, used it constantly at night, and took it in the car everywhere we went. Other kids played with toy guns or toy trucks. I played with my flashlight.

On this particular occasion our family of five had just nestled into our sleeping bags for the night. After dad turned the Coleman lantern off, we used my flashlight to get settled in. Even though it wasn't needed beyond that, I continued to flick it off and on . . . off and on . . . off and on . . . you get the idea.

Finally my dad had enough and said, "Okay, son, let's not turn the flashlight on any more; it's time to go to sleep."

Almost two whole minutes passed before I simply couldn't resist the urge to disobey.

Click.

The entire tent lit up like the noon-day sun. I was even surprised with how bright it was.

"Timothy *Dryden!* I said turn the flashlight *off*—and *leave* it off," my dad barked.

One of my brothers whispered a warning to me about the certainty of a forthcoming whipping if I didn't obey. My dad was a strict disciplinarian, so spankings happened fairly regularly, sometimes hourly, in my case. My dad never subscribed to the, "Okay, you better do what I say or I'm gonna count to three!" method of training. It was either do what he said, when he said it, or immediately experience repercussions.

This time, I guess about seven or eight minutes passed. (You know where this story is heading, don't you?) I honestly can't remember if it was willful disobedience, rank stupidity, or simply an accident, but I continued to fiddle with my trusty flashlight and . . . *click*.

My dad, understandably, snapped. That last *click* popped his patience bubble. Before he could yell at me, I quickly realized what I had done, and turned it off. I could feel the tension in the dark tent. I could see the headlines now: "Eight Year Old Boy Chokes On Flashlight".

My dad growled impatiently, "If you turn that flashlight on ONE. MORE. TIME. I'm gonna . . ."

To my misfortune, I honestly thought he said, "Turn that flashlight on *one more time.*"

So, being the obedient child I was, I did just as he instructed.
Click.

To this day, I'm not quite sure how both of us survived. Either my dad was about to have a heart attack, or I was about to be mauled, or perhaps he would have a heart attack while mauling me. As soon as the "click" happened *again*, and the entire tent illumined, my dad began scrambling furiously from his sleeping bag, trying to get to me. It reminded me of that story from Sunday school about King Nebuchadnezzar turning into a wild beast. I was in *big* trouble.

Fortunately, three bodies separated him from his object of wrath— me. My oldest brother grabbed him around the neck, while my other brother wrapped his arms around his legs. They were concerned about my chances for survival and began frantically telling him that I thought he had told me to turn it on one more time. That I had misunderstood him. That I was too young to die.

My dad stopped struggling to get to me. The silence was broken by a slight giggle from my mom. Then one of my brothers made that snorting noise with his nose that we all make when we're trying hard to suppress a laugh. Then came the sweetest sound I've ever heard. My dad began laughing hysterically.

Hallelujah! I would live to see many more campgrounds after all. But to this day, I always hesitate for a second before flicking on a flashlight.

A Popped Patience Bubble

S ERVING AS TOUR DIRECTOR for a bunch of ballerinas and balledudes can be trying at times. Artists in general, and ballet dancers in particular, have a great deal of trouble focusing on bothersome details like what time it is, what day it is, what month it is, what city or state they are currently in, and where they are going next. It's not a matter of intellect, but one of interest. They're often clueless as to what time they need to *start* getting ready because their interest in following schedules is comparable to my West Highland Terrier's interest in the six o'clock news. Simply put, dancers don't get gray hair worrying about schedules of any kind except when their next ballet class begins.

My job was not only to book our programs, but then to get the eleven of us from city to city during our tour and, when possible, to arrive at more or less the time I had prearranged with the sponsor. It's a constant struggle to spend my time wisely when we're off the road, alternating between booking future tours and arranging the myriad of details for the next trip.

On one occasion, I was having a particularly stressful time preparing to depart for our Texas tour the next day because of two recent cancellations. Our child had kept me up most of the previous night, there was a steady stream of interruptions in my office, and all of the sponsors that I needed to contact were impossible to reach. I was tired, irritated, and frustrated. My ever-thinning bubble of patience was about to pop. Then a six-foot-tall needle walked into my office.

One of the dancers, John Vandervelde, approached me somewhat hesitantly with a sheepish look on his face. John and I roomed together on tour prior to my marriage to Deana, and I consider him to be one of my all-time closest friends. "Tim, I meant to tell you this earlier, but my family and I borrowed the bus a couple of weeks ago and at some point during our trip, the air conditioner stopped working."

This popped my patience bubble. I was in disbelief. We were leaving in less than twenty-four hours for El Paso, Texas, whose weatherman had boasted of a "cooling trend" for the next day back down into the upper 90s with humidity at about the same number. We were scheduled to leave the next morning at seven o'clock for the hottest state in the nation, during the hottest month of the year, in a forty-foot-long *oven* on wheels! Furthermore, you usually have to make an appointment to get maintenance done on a bus—you don't just pop in to a garage somewhere and add some Freon.

John calmly walked out of the room and into the studio, picked up his guitar, and began leading the other dancers in worship. The fact that he wasn't fretting about the situation at all frustrated me even more.

Keith Thibodeaux had witnessed his confession and was also annoyed, but not nearly as angry as I was. "Can you believe it?!" Keith exclaimed. "Why didn't he tell us before today? I just can't believe it!"

I was *livid*. "YOU can't believe it?! I can't believe it either!" I shouted, as I buried my fist into a three-ring binder lying on top of my desk.

Keith encouraged me to calm down and suggested we go immediately and see about getting the air conditioner repaired. I drove the bus and followed Keith to the shop. On the way there I noticed something really scary. The side of my hand—the one I had used as an instrument of unrighteousness by slamming it into my booking binder—had swollen to hideous proportions. It looked like there was a golf ball under the skin on my pinky-finger knuckle. There was something seriously wrong with my hand—maybe a broken bone or something, but I was too embarrassed at the time to tell Keith.

Later that day, Deana and I went to our company doctor's office. Dr. Sam Fillingane, whose office at that time was in Forest, Mississippi, treated the members of our ministry, either at no-charge or at an extremely reduced rate. He knew that none of us had health insurance and considered treating us to be his ministry. He was out of town when I went in, but the nurses X-rayed my hand and said it was badly fractured in a couple of places and would almost certainly need surgery. They wanted to schedule the surgery for the *next morning*.

I couldn't believe what I was hearing. That simply was not possible. We were leaving on tour at 8:00 a.m. the *next morning*. It would create a logistical nightmare if I had to miss the first few days of tour! I'm the Tour *Director!* I help drive the bus, coordinate our schedule, and unload over one-ton of equipment from our bus for each program. Then I help set everything up and operate our lighting and sound equipment. I also introduce the dancers from the microphone and make announcements. If we were leaving in a week or two, arrangements could be made, but we were leaving the next day.

My outburst of anger had caused a big problem. I was sorely convicted and completely humiliated. I'm in full-time ministry and had broken my hand in unbridled anger. Deana, Keith, Kathy, and everybody else would be really disappointed in me. Thousands of people in audiences across several states were going to see me onstage with a cast like a neon sign flashing *I'm an idiot, I'm an idiot, I'm an idiot.* Then there was the added misery of anxiety—where was the $2,000 needed for surgery going to come from? And the guilt that it was needed in the first place. I had messed up real bad.

The Artist was going to have to be extremely creative to get me out of this one. I knew well his promise: "My grace is sufficient for you, for my power is made perfect in weakness." But surely he had included a disclaimer for morons in full-time ministry who break their hands in anger. If I were God, I definitely would not have helped me.

One of the nurses already had the phone in her hand to schedule the surgery, but I motioned for her not to make the call. I explained to her my role on tour and asked if there was *any way* to take care of my hand at a later date. It was at this point that I remember hoping she would say something like, "Well, let's see, we could just shoot you. That's what you deserve!" But she smiled patiently at me—the same look my wife used to give our newborn children when they would spit up on her.

"Let me call the surgeon's office and see if they think this can wait for a week or two." I was relieved when they agreed to wait until I returned from tour, saying that the swelling would have gone down by then. The nurses put a splint on my hand, gave me some medication for pain, and sent me on my way. We sat in silence as

Deana drove me back home. By the time I arrived at the bus the next morning, my hand was really swollen and painful.

God began to orchestrate a remarkable set of circumstances that only he could have done. Five days into the tour, we were eating dinner with our host family following a program in Fort Worth, Texas. The man of the house, David, asked me how I had hurt my hand. After I told him the embarrassing account of how it happened, he asked me a puzzling question.

"Do you happen to have the X-rays with you?" he asked.

I wondered why he would be interested in whether or not I had them. "Yes, sir, I don't really know why I brought them, but they're on the bus, under my bunk to keep them flat. Why, are you in the medical profession?"

All four of his children and his wife smiled when I asked that question. "David is a medical doctor and has a busy family practice here in Fort Worth," his wife explained. She went on to say that he had specialized in orthopedics during his stint in the Army.

The doctor then casually suggested that after dinner he drive me to the bus so he could take a look at the X-rays. "I expect I can fix you up tonight if you like."

"What exactly do you mean, 'fix me up'?"

He responded very matter-of-factly. "Well, depending on what it looks like, I can go ahead and set it for you tonight, and you can come by the office in the morning, and I'll cast it for you."

I was so thankful. It was another God-ordained coincidence that I just happened to be staying at an orthopedic surgeon's home. After dinner he drove me to the bus, we boarded, and he followed me to my bunk. He began to think aloud as he held the X-rays up to the dome light.

"Uh huh . . . uh huh . . . yep, I think I can set this so that you won't even need surgery."

When we got back to his house, the doctor told me to have a seat at the kitchen counter. He offered me a little brandy before starting the painful process of deadening my hand so that he could set it. In keeping with my macho image, I declined his offer with a confident smile. Dr. Capper then opened the refrigerator and removed what looked like an eight-penny nail protruding from a syringe! It looked like it belonged in a veterinarian's office! I honestly thought he was joking me. Unfortunately, he wasn't.

I gulped hard, but managed to say, "You know, on second thought, I believe I *will* have just a touch of that brandy after all."

It was at this point that he offered that clichéd pseudo-warning that all doctors and nurses apparently learn early in the educational process: "Now this might sting a little." As he rubbed my hand with an alcohol-drenched cotton ball, my eyes were riveted to the two-foot-long needle and I thought, *You know, I bet he's right, it just might sting a little.*

Dr. Capper then commenced the enjoyable process of numbing my hand. Very little that I could read in the Bible would serve as a deterrent to future outbursts of anger quite as well as the "little sting" I was now experiencing. He then held my arm up parallel to the ground, took my little finger and ring finger into his hands, and instructed me to play tug-o-war with him, to resist him as he pulled on my hand so that he could set the bones back in order. It sounded like Rice Krispies through an amplifier with all the snap! crackle! and pop! going on. Imagine an entire soccer team cracking their knuckles at once. The doctor had it set in a couple of minutes, wrapped it in an Ace bandage, warned me not to remove the bandage for *any* reason (any reason!), and sent me to bed.

Upon arrival at Dr. Capper's office the following morning, I was whisked past all the other patients in the waiting room to X-ray. The technician reminded me a bit of my own mom as she tenderly began to unravel the Ace bandage from my hand. I pulled my hand back from her momentarily, and told her I didn't think the doctor wanted her to remove the bandage, because he had set it the night before. She assured me that it was routine procedure because sometimes the butterfly clips give a false picture.

Guess what? She was right; it was *normally* routine procedure. But in this *abnormal* case, when the attending physician himself had set the bone the night before, she should not have taken my hand out of the bandage. The way the bones were set was very unstable and they fell out of place again. He was going to have to reset it. *Whoopee!*

This time the atmosphere was not so relaxed, we were not in a kitchen all alone; there were patients waiting to see the doctor, and there was no brandy *anywhere*. Dr. Capper hurriedly grabbed another syringe, reminded me that it might sting a little, then quickly repeated the painful process. This time he didn't have all day to wait for the drug to take effect before re-setting my hand. It was as though God wanted to be sure that I never again slammed my fist down in anger.

Dr. Capper was quite the craftsman when it came to casting my hand. He made me clench an entire roll of gauze in the palm of my hand, then carefully fashioned a cast around it, leaving my thumb and forefinger just enough freedom to get some use out of them. I was then sent back to have it X-rayed again to ensure that the bones were lined up properly.

The Artist in me was still orchestrating everything through this entire debacle. The same technician was taking these X-rays, and she apologized profusely for the extra pain I had just endured due to her mistake. I assured her that it was I who should be apologizing for taking up so many professionals' time because I had broken my hand in anger.

During this second trip to be X-rayed, I started thinking that this woman was troubled about one of her children. I checked to see if she was wearing a wedding band. She wasn't. My brain (about the size of an English pea) began logically concluding that this woman had probably never even been married, much less had children. What if I asked her if she was particularly concerned this morning for one of her children, and she burst into tears, saying all she ever wanted was to be married and have a family? My heart started beating that goofy way it does when I know I have to do something that's scary.

"Ma'am, uh, may I tell you—or, uh, ask you something?"

"Well, of course, son, what is it?"

"I hesitate to ask you this because . . . well, as I've been sitting here I started thinking that you're really worried about one of your children, and I'd love to pray for you if that's true."

I don't think I'll ever forget the look on that woman's face. She locked eyes with me, slowly backed up to a chair in the corner, and slowly sat down. "Are you a minister?" I explained to her that I sorta-kinda was (you can use non-words like "sorta-kinda" in Texas, especially if you're from Mississippi), but that I was not an ordained, preach-every-Sunday kind of minister. Big tears welled up in her eyes as she explained to me that, *just the night before*, her daughter had called from several states away and shocked her with the news that her marriage—to a pastor—was crumbling. I told her I'd pray for her and she insisted that we call her daughter immediately to let her know that God was keenly aware of her plight and that this was a tangible sign from him that his grace is sufficient and his power is perfected in our weakness.

Once on the phone with her daughter, she related to her what I had just asked, then handed the phone to me. I prayed with her over the phone about what she was experiencing, and by the time we hung up, she was noticeably encouraged.

On the way out of town that afternoon, I thought through everything that had happened. Only the Master Artist could have woven such an intricate pattern of circumstances together for our benefit and his glory.

In a metropolis the size of Fort Worth, Texas, I just *happened* to stay in the home of a medical doctor who just *happened* to have received orthopedic training. I just *happened* to have the X-rays with me on tour, and this particular physician just *happened* to be willing to drive to our bus about midnight, even though he had clinic the next morning. He was then also willing to work on my hand until after 2:00 o'clock in the morning! And out of hundreds of people who work in X-ray labs in that area, I *happened* to be cared for by a woman whose daughter needed a reminder of how loving our heavenly Father really is.

Either I'm one of the luckiest people on earth (in which case I need to skedaddle on over to Vegas), or, more likely, the Artist's love and creative genius is beyond measure!

How Can You Not Have A Fan?

S O THERE WE WERE—back in the Lone Star state, this time staying in the beautiful home of a psychiatrist in Woodlands, Texas. His name—and I kid you not—was Dr. Looney. Yes, seriously. "Honey, will you pick up the kids today? I have a counseling appointment with Dr. Looney." I digress.

Here are three of the more memorable "homestays".

A couple in their 30s with two beautiful children complimented my wife on the beauty of the program as we walked to their late model suburban with our luggage, pop-up crib, and four-year-old son in tow. They spoke fondly of their home state of Illinois and were amused to hear of backstage foibles that had transpired during the performance that evening. After feeding us a delicious meal, the couple grabbed our luggage to serve us and began leading us upstairs to our bedroom for the night.

The man of the house opened the door and walked in to the far side of their smallish guest bedroom, his wife followed, and the three of us entered as well. The man set down the luggage, clasped his hands together sort of in the prayer position, and with a big smile said, "Again, we are so blessed to have you with us tonight. Please let us know if you need *anything*." (Note the emphasis on *anything*).

He and his wife stepped out and gently pulled the door shut behind them. Deana and I looked at each other, and her expression was priceless. She was smiling but every bit as confused as I was. The room was a perfectly normal guest bedroom, and it was spotlessly clean. But, there was one, glaring problem—it was empty. Real empty. I'm talking *completely* empty, as was the nice walk-in closet. And when I say *empty*, I mean there was no bed, no chair, no chest of drawers or furniture of any kind—nothing. There were no clothes or clothes hangers in the closet. It looked like a room in a home that had been on the market for a month after the owners vacated the premises. There was a hardwood floor, oh, and nice blinds covering the window for privacy. Mathias was perfectly comfortable in his pop-up crib after Deana put her foot down about me trying to fit in it for the night. I suppose it wasn't even close to as difficult as eating grub worms in Africa or something. Unless maybe they were cooked in a crockpot and smothered with onions.

Needless to say, we survived the night to tell the tale. I think everyone should try to sleep on hardwood floors at least once in their lives. It builds character . . . and definitely makes for good dinner conversation. At the very least, you will never hear the story of Jacob sleeping in the wilderness with a stone for a pillow without a greater appreciation for his sacrifice.

ONCE AFTER A PROGRAM in New England we left the theatre with our hostess, a single mom in her 40s and drove 45 miles to her home. Our son cried loudly for, oh, only about 44 of those miles, even though Deana tried everything in her power to comfort the tired little baby. We had boarded the bus at 7:30 that morning, drove 300 miles, set up our equipment, the dancers took a 90-minute class, then a two-hour program, followed by the requisite one-hour strike of our equipment. We arrived at her home just shy of midnight, and as she was unlocking her front door, she gave us a friendly warning that she had a really sweet but very active springer spaniel puppy on the other side of the door quivering with excitement to meet our little family. Deana and I didn't share the dog's excitement; we just wanted to get our baby in his pop-up crib, give him his bottle, and crash. We were unusually exhausted.

As soon as we stepped in to her foyer her dog accosted us with the friendliness of an over-excited (and perhaps lovesick) dog and only stopped jumping on both of us to thrust his snout in some very personal places of Deana, whose only defense, because both of her hands were tied up with holding the baby, was to twirl and turn to escape his prying snout. She had done enough twirling and turning for the day already. If that wasn't bad enough, then the precious pooch thought he would explore my unique smells, perhaps as an educational activity—sort of like a field trip. Our hostess had turned her back to us and was walking toward the kitchen, so I reached down and depressed his left eyeball with my thumb—very lovingly, of course. When his moan almost elevated to a yelp, I released and he ran into another room. (Fear not: no dog was hurt in the retelling of this story).

As she began gathering ingredients out of the refrigerator to make dinner, she motioned across the kitchen counter to the living room couch, and told us it makes out into a bed. That wasn't unusual, but we knew there might be fireworks later because that's also where the dog slept. As we visited with the woman we discovered she was an amazing portrait of God's grace and strength, and had come through some very difficult times. She was extremely hospitable and loving. As we were saying goodnight at 1:05 a.m., she lamented the fact that she and her daughter had to leave at 5:00 a.m., and she assured us they would try to be quiet making breakfast in the kitchen. We were lamenting her early departure too.

Three things happened simultaneously at 4:15 a.m. A stainless steel pot destined for use in cooking oatmeal accidentally fell to the floor from an overhead rack in the kitchen, Mathias started wailing uncontrollably, and a loving dog's tongue began feverishly licking my entire face. Suddenly, I was reminded of a church secretary in Phoenix, who was munching on a bag of Cheetos as we gathered in the church foyer before heading to the next venue. Between bites she asked me where we were going next, and after I told her she said, "Must be nice. Some of us have to work for a living." That didn't make me think kind thoughts, of course. I was thinking how much I would like to take that bag of Cheetos and . . .

Yes, must be nice.

FOR EVERY BAD OR uncomfortable homestay we experienced, we probably had 20 wonderful stays. There are so many unbelievably gracious, generous, and hospitable people across this great country. But none were any more enjoyable than Larry and Dixie Torrech of Virginia Beach, Virginia. We were scheduled for a program at Kempsville Presbyterian Church in Virginia Beach, and they had volunteered to accommodate us. Both of their daughters, Rachel and Rebecca, loved ballet and took classes and were no doubt looking forward to having two, real, live ballerina's actually sleeping in their home. Deana wasn't on this trip because she was in the latter months of pregnancy, so this precious but unsuspecting family landed me and John Vandervelde, a

35-year-old male dancer and a rather large *non*-dancer from Mississippi, as their guests for the evening.

Woohoo. I'm sure their daughters were just thrilled.

I know you'll find this hard to believe, but I really like to tell stories—especially personal, funny stories. My stories were amusing Dixie, and she was matching me story for story! She was hilarious to John and me. My favorite was something that happened to a choir director who had spoken at her church recently.

He related that he and his wife were running terribly late while getting ready to go to a formal banquet. The stress had caused them to start bickering with each other about something altogether unimportant, but they were getting increasingly angry with one another. As the choir director continued he admitted it was embarrassing to expose their impatience with each other with all those at the retreat, but that it was worth it. While arguing and hurrying to get ready, she turned her back to him and said, "Just shut up, and zip me up." He impishly took hold of her zipper, and zipped it up and down really fast 3 times just to annoy her. The zipper broke, making his wife appropriately *livid.* There wasn't time for her to change her entire outfit, so she covered the broken zipper with a scarf which she didn't really like to begin with. But when other women kept looking at it with a confused looks and offering what she deemed to be insincere compliments, she was further annoyed.

The next morning as she stormed past her husband on her way out of the house she told him she was going shopping to buy two dresses because of what had happened with her favorite dress the night before. Three hours later she got home with her two new dresses and walked up the driveway past her husband as he was working underneath their car. He was lying on his back and was under the car from his waist up. As she walked past him, she reached down, grabbed the zipper of his pants, and zipped it up and down three times. He flinched, and she walked in the house with a smile of satisfaction.

As she was walking through the living room, her husband lowered the paper he was reading, and asked, "So did you get your two dresses of vengeance?"

She wheeled around in shocked horror. "Oh my *gosh!* Who's that out there working on our car?"

"Fred. He thinks he'll have it done by lunch."

"I just grabbed the zipper on his pants and zipped it up and down, because I thought it was you! You've got to go explain to him why I grabbed his zipper."

He laughed at her predicament. "I'm not going to bail you out— you shouldn't have done it in the first place."

So she went out to the car, got on her knees so she could explain to Fred face-to-face how sorry she was. His forehead had a big, dark, greasy spot on it, and he seemed like he was just waking up. He was the first one to speak. "It was the weirdest thing ever. Some person just walked up from the street and grabbed my zipper and zipped it back and forth. It totally caught me by surprise and I jerked up and hit my head on the underside of the car. He continued as he was rubbing his forehead, "I guess I knocked myself out."

"Wow. Are you kidding me?" she asked. "Did you get a good look at who it was?"

"Not at all. I have no idea."

"I'm so sorry that happened, can I get you anything?"

Hilarious story.

But, as with all good things, they must end. So when we finished relating stories, Dixie asked if she could get me anything before we turned in for the night. I told her I would love to borrow a box fan, or any kind of oscillating fan for the night, because I love to keep the air stirring. Plus, the "white noise" helps me sleep better. She told me they didn't have a fan. I said I'm sure you guys have some kind of fan, maybe out in the garage or in the attic. She smiled one of those I'm-sure-you'll-be-fine-without-a-fan-for-one-night smiles, and assured me that she was quite aware of what they had and didn't have, and she was sure they didn't have a fan.

I took this as license to poke fun at her about this odd fact. "What normal American with a two-story house doesn't have a fan? Are you *kidding* me?"

She playfully snapped back. "What normal American requires a box fan to fall asleep?"

We both laughed and called it a night.

Fast forward 24 years. As I was walking from table to table at a Sunday picnic at the new church to which I was called to be the assistant pastor, a petite and cheery woman rushed up to me with a large photograph album. She had opened it to the page she wanted me to see. "Do you recognize this handwriting?"

Of course I did—it was *my* handwriting after all. Dixie Torrech, the fun Virginia Beach hostess explained how she thought I looked familiar, but couldn't quite put her finger on how or from where she knew me. It had, after all, been nearly a quarter century, but what a joyful surprise reunion it was.

Real Estate Roulette

IT WAS PART OF KATHY'S vision from the very beginning. She dreamed of dancing for the honor of God with other professionals, but she also wanted to see a School of the Arts developed to help train the next generation. We had been touring as a performing company for about four years, but now it was time to open a school. It was not a breeze to open such a school. Some of the required ingredients were: quite a bit of money, several qualified dance teachers willing to work for next to nothing, and to secure a sizeable building to serve as the studio. And, not to mention, we needed students—paying students, to be exact. Oh, and the building needed to be, well, ridiculously inexpensive.

Reasoning that it might be a selling point to potential teachers if we actually had a studio, we decided to search for that piece of the puzzle first. After checking out many properties which either seemed low quality or creepy or both, or properties that had potential, but would need a massive amount of re-modeling, we finally found what seemed like a near-perfect spot. It was a *Gold's Gym* that had moved out of a strip shopping center located on a well-travelled road near downtown Jackson, Mississippi.

It had large, open rooms with mirrors lining the walls in two different rooms. There were two large dressing rooms and nice bathrooms. There was just one problem. After discussing the issue with some financially wise friends, we decided that we *might* be able to afford about $2 per square foot for rent, *if*—and that's a big *if*—we could get deposits for enrollment from at least 150 students from the initial start-up of the school.

The owner of the shopping center was a friendly, but very business-like gentleman who lived in Miami. He had told us he would like to rent that particular space for $8 per square foot, but was willing to consider a "reasonable offer". As we began discussions with him, the dancers left for a tour in Hawaii which turned out to be an amazing adventure as well. But that left me as the only company member to try to negotiate a deal to rent studio space. I knew I was in way over my head, not knowing the first thing about real estate dealings. So I called a close friend and major supporter of Ballet Magnificat, Homer Lee Howie.

Mr. Howie, or Homer Lee, as he prefers, has what northerners would call a thick Southern drawl, and he is a business genius. He is a very successful investor, primarily in the area of real estate. So I contacted him and he was more than happy to help us any way he could. When I asked him if he would call the owner of the shopping center and try to negotiate a deal for us he said, "Naw, but I'll do something even better. I'll coach *you* to negotiate the deal."

"Homer Lee you don't understand. I know about as much about real estate deals as I know about the dental hygiene habits of piranhas."

"Well, I don't know, I figure that's what makes you the perfect man for the job, and I'll help you. He'll recognize real quick, if he hasn't already, that you don't know the first thing about it. I figure that might work in our favor in a couple of ways. First, if a legitimate agent or investor made him the offer you're gonna make him, it would rile him up like a rattlesnake poked with a branding iron. But he'll figure you don't know any better. Second, he might just bite on our offer because dealing with you will keep pride from playing into it so much. Men like him are used to playing hardball with rich folks all day, every day. They'll say no to deals that would make them money just because they don't want to appear weak to other investors. Your ignorance of the system will sorta give him permission to maybe wiggle a little bit with us. You understand what I'm saying, son?"

I didn't totally grasp his plan yet, but I did understand that Homer Lee is crazy like a fox when it comes to brokering deals. So the first thing he told me to do was to draw up a proposal and make it look as professional as I could, and offer him $3 a square foot in writing. The owner, Mr. Rosen, was Jewish, and as Homer Lee pointed out, was "smart as a whip". I found out later that Homer Lee was counting on my proposal looking pretty close to pitiful (gee thanks for the confidence). He told me to fax it to the entrepreneur in Miami, and to not argue with him *at all* when he called me up mad as a hornet in about 30 minutes. "Tim, just hear him out, apologize for the offer, and tell him you'll get back to him with a better offer tomorrow. Then call me."

All this had me worried. "Homer Lee, that's already a dollar more per square foot than we can possibly afford, so how in the world can I make him a better offer tomorrow?"

"I 'magine I've done this kind of thing a time or two more than you have son. God is a fair Broker himself, and he's steered me through many a good deal through the years. I 'spect he'll help us on this thing too."

I can't believe I questioned his judgment. Maybe I could offer Tiger Woods some advice on his golf swing as well. How embarrassing.

So I hung up and prepared the best proposal I could: I offered $3 per square foot, and faxed it to his office in Miami, just as I was instructed. In about 30 minutes my office phone rung. (Wait, isn't that when Homer Lee said he would call)? The voice on the other end was the owner's. He politely asked, "Is this Mr. Dryden?" That was the last polite thing he said. He used *very* descriptive language regarding what he thought about my offer, and even had some ideas about what I could do with it. He barked at me for less than a minute. When he stopped, I just apologized and told him I'd get back to him with a better offer as Homer Lee had instructed me.

Then I called Mr. Howie for further instruction. He told me to call him back the next day at 3:35 p.m. our time which would be 4:35 p.m. in Miami, because the owner would probably be thinking that he wasn't going to hear from me after all. So he would be more likely to be glad to hear from me. I was to explain that I would make another offer momentarily, but first I had a few things for him to consider. Mr. Howie coached me how to remind Mr. Rosen that all of the businesses located in the strip mall had been faithful to stay there even though the economy had slowed. And if the ballet studio moved in, it would draw at least 150 parents and kids there *every week* from the day we opened. That would drastically increase traffic and potential business to the mall. It would also increase the property value since the 3,000-square-foot studio was the largest single space in the strip mall, and it had been vacant for months. If there was more business generated because of our presence, it would be better for him *and* all of the other merchants. It would be a win-win situation.

Then I was to tell him that we were prepared to offer him $4 per square foot, but that we would need him to make a tax deductible donation to our non-profit organization for the equivalent of $2 per square foot monthly, and then we would send him the $4 per square foot. So I called him up at 4:35 p.m. his time, and told him everything just as I was instructed.

There was a moment of silence as he was processing all of this. "So let me get this straight. You're suggesting that I pay $2 a square foot and you pay $2 a square foot monthly for *my property?*

"Not exactly sir. You probably could use some tax relief, so I'm suggesting we pay you $4 a square foot monthly, and you make a charitable donation to our non-profit arts organization monthly."

More silence. Then I heard unintelligible whispering, followed by, "I'll have to call you tomorrow Mr. Dryden."

It would not be completely untruthful to say that I did not truly expect him to call—at least with any good news, that is. But genuinely peculiar events were happening to us all the time (and outta the blue), so I should've learned by now who was in my corner and trust the most savvy Broker of all.

Anyway, the next day he called and said he would not take the deal at $4 a square foot. My optimism disappeared. I knew it was too good to be true. But then something extraordinary happened. He continued by telling me that he was raising the rent to $5 a square foot . . . and—here's the best part—he would donate $3 a square foot to us monthly!

We took the deal, most assuredly. And the Broker sent the students. We opened the studio with 180 students, enough to pay our portion of the rent and pay the teachers and director of the school. The wisest Negotiator in existence had artfully crafted a plan and executed it to perfection.

Rutherford's Unforgettable Problem

S EVERAL TIMES THROUGHOUT our years with Ballet Magnificat my wife Deana and I had to be separated for a few weeks for one reason or another. On one such occasion she was in a latter month of pregnancy, and I travelled while she stayed home. My roommate for one particular homestay was our fantastic male dancer from the Czech Republic, Jiri Voborsky. He would later marry Cassandra Piotrowski, a beautiful dancer and extremely hard worker from Jarrettsville, Maryland. But this was prior to their marriage, so he had the unforgettable honor of being able to room with me for one night in Connecticut.

It was a gorgeous home in a very upscale neighborhood, and the owners, a couple in their 40s, were terrific hosts. Jiri and I arrived at their home late at night, sometime around 11:30 p.m., and we were served delicious soup and salad on fine china. The man owned a large shipping company and actually offered to fly me down to Atlanta with him the next night on the company leer jet to watch the Braves play, but I was forced to decline, because we had another program in another city the next night. Rats!

He was still wearing his suit and tie from his day at the office, and she sported a beautiful cashmere sweater and diamond necklace. While we were eating, their large, brown, well-groomed Golden Retriever, Rutherford, sauntered into the room quietly. He sat down, and looked up at the woman of the house with his beautiful brown eyes. She looked at him and determined quickly that something was wrong. "Oh honey," she said to her husband, "Rutherford is freezing. Can you adjust the temperature please?"

Jiri and I kept eating our soup as the man exited the room.

He returned and sounded somewhat concerned, "No wonder. It was set to 73 degrees; I changed it to 74."

Jiri and I exchanged glances at each other in disbelief. We continued chatting until about 5 minutes later, when Rutherford, who by all accounts looked *perfectly* content, let out a barely detectible moan. It seemed like an "ahh-this-is-the-life" kind of moan to me and Jiri. It was the same kind of moan I make after I've eaten too much on Thanksgiving, as I'm falling back on the couch to watch football. But we obviously had *completely* misinterpreted his faintly audible moan. What do we know? We don't even have a dog, so clearly we were not in a position to make any sort of assessment about canines. Better leave that to the experts.

"Oh no! He's starving, honey. I ran out of the prime rib, but I think we still have some roast beef left."

Realizing both delicacies she had just mentioned for Rutherford were better fare than the chicken noodle soup we were enjoying, she explained that she knew we would just want something light after the program. They then told us that they had to send Rutherford to obedience school when he was a puppy, because he was hurting their marriage. "Honey" had become sick and tired of things like the time Rutherford destroyed a $12,000 oriental rug in their den. Then there was the incident of the marinating chicken breasts. In the time it took the woman to retrieve their dry cleaning at the front door, Rutherford had caused 8 boneless chicken breasts to disappear. *Eight!* Assuming he couldn't have devoured all 8 in the allotted time it took her to make a round trip to the front door, she searched high and low for where he might have hidden the ones he didn't consume. She still hasn't found them.

Reminiscing about Rutherford's earlier days prompted the woman to ask her husband if she could tell us *the* story. He smiled and nodded in agreement. She began the story with this sentence. "One day I was washing dishes here at the sink and noticed Rutherford in the backyard doing his business." Jiri had never heard of a dog "doing his business". But he figured it out soon enough. She continued. "He was sort of hunched over, you know, that way they do when they are going to the bathroom?" I nodded that I understood, and Jiri and I both thought it a good time to end our meals.

"Well, I could tell he was struggling. So I put on my dishwashing gloves and went out to see if I could help him."

Um, yep. That's what she said. Those were her exact words, one of the more memorable quotes I ever heard as I travelled around the nation. And it came from such an unlikely source. I couldn't believe my ears. I could understand if we had finished eating hours earlier, and had enjoyed maybe one too many glasses of wine . . . wait, no. I still couldn't understand it even then.

It gets better. She held up her hand and made a pinching motion with her thumb and forefinger to demonstrate for us exactly how she "helped" Rutherford. "So I grabbed it, and started gently pulling it out, and it just kept coming and coming and coming . . ." Then, both she and "honey" laughed loudly through the punchline of the story—insert drumroll here—"It was an entire, intact pair of my pantyhose!"

Jiri and I helped clean up after we threw up on her fancy kitchen table before retiring for the night. No, we didn't actually throw up, surprisingly, and, yes, it was funny to us later. Much later.

Taste Buds, Man

THE ONE MAN WHO probably brought the most laughter and joy to many of the earliest company members is a man named James Arnold from Satsuma, Alabama. I'm as sure as I can be without interviewing them, that the following Ballet Magnificat pioneers would agree with this claim about James: Keith and Kathy Thibodeaux, Michael and Mary Cadle, Rick and Rose Faucher, Laura Bremer Faucher, John and Karin Vandervelde, Jeff and Heidi Bieber, Jiri and Cassandra Piotrowski, Christina Hudson, and James' wife, Wendy Witchow, a former ballerina with the company.

James saw the company perform at the University of Southern Alabama, and simply fell in love with the ballet . . . as a whole. He wanted to spend as much time with the company as he possibly could, he wanted to travel with the company and help out any way possible. James has a heart as big as Texas, especially for "any poor soul who doesn't know God." He shamelessly proclaims his beliefs anywhere, at any time, and to anyone who will listen. James grew up in near poverty in the metropolis of Satsuma in Alabama, population 5,700, and so, naturally, he was a little rough around the edges. There are more stories than I will share now, but here is just a taste of some of the stories which come from our relationship with this hilarious and precious man.

When he first moved to Jackson to be near the company I let him stay in my home with me. I was single, and it seemed foolish for him to stay anywhere else. We used to love standing in my little kitchen while eating our late night snacks, discussing whatever life threw at us that day. James really liked toast, well actually he *loved* toast, particularly if it was completely concealed in jelly. Lots of cold, grape jelly, to be exact. One night he was particularly animated as he recounted his interaction that day with Wendy, his future wife. You know most people—the normal ones, anyway—put a small glob of jelly in the middle of a piece of toast, and then spread it around to nicely cover the entire piece of bread. James didn't follow this norm. James put a little glob in the center like everybody does, but then he added 5 or 6 more globs all over the toast. But, if you think about it, it is actually quite brilliant. By slopping jelly over ever spare inch of toast, that bypasses the need to spread the jelly. I could live with this, and I could live with the resulting need to purchase several jars of grape jelly monthly, but I couldn't live with how he ate the toast, and the mess this caused.

After burying his toast with grape jelly—big, loose, mounds of grape jelly—James would turn the bread *upside down* to eat it. What are you thinking happened when he turned it upside down to consume it? Yep, some (a lot) of those jelly globs fell off and landed on his shirtless belly, and then gravity would cause the excess jelly to roll downward, but of course it couldn't make the turn with of the contour of his stomach, and it would fall on my kitchen floor. (Think slooow-motion here). When I frowned and pointed to the jelly on the floor, James grabbed a napkin, never slowed down telling his story, and made sort of a swirling motion at the jelly on the floor, as if it was a cleaning product he was rubbing *into* the floor, not wiping up *from* the floor. He got only about half of the jelly on the napkin, but hey, that left a visually stunning purple pattern on the floor.

At this point, I had had enough. "Brother you're making such a mess. Can't you feel the globs of jelly rolling down your stomach?" I held out my toast to demonstrate. "Why don't you let gravity be your friend, and hold your toast like this, you know, the side with the jelly on it facing upward and a lot of that jelly will actually get in your mouth? So why do you eat it jelly side down?"

Without missing a beat, he said in all sincerity, "Taste buds, man. You ain't got no taste buds on the roof of your mouth."

How could I stay mad at that?

ANOTHER INCIDENT INVOLVING food and James happened one night when I had invited a friend (of the female variety) over for dinner. James thought it was a really big deal for me, like a really important, pull-all-the-stops-out date with a marriage prospect. I assured him repeatedly that she was just a good buddy, and we were just going to eat a bite and watch a movie. No big deal. I even told him he was more than welcome to join us if he wanted to. He just laughed a sinister laugh and assured me that he wouldn't come home that evening until after 1:00 a.m. to give us "all the privacy we could possibly want". I assured him once again that my friend and I needed *no* privacy, and that all the doors and drapes would be wide open, and some of our other friends might show up as well.

I finally stopped trying to convince him. The last thing he said as he left for the evening was that he wanted to hear about the date when he got home early the next morning. And then he hit me with his best shot at a comedic zinger. "Don't do anything I wouldn't do."

And with that he left.

My friend (who happened to be a girl) and I had finished eating dinner and were about an hour into the movie when James came in and headed to the kitchen. It was only 10 'til 8 (yes, 7:50 p.m.), and mister-I-won't-see-you-'til-way-after-midnight began loudly rummaging through my pantry. I had warned my friend about James, that he could be . . . well, eccentric sometimes. He yelled a question from the kitchen.

"Hey Tim, where in the world are the saltines? Are you out? Tell me we're not out of saltines."

I shouted back that if we had any they would be on the middle shelf with the cereal. I explained to my friend that he was referring to is what most of us call "crackers". We heard him searching feverishly for another couple of minutes, and then he came into the living room, and as he approached us sitting together on the couch, he introduced himself to my friend. But it didn't stop there. He proceeded to sit down between us on the couch—no joke—with a small jar of mayonnaise in one hand and an oversized spoon in the other.

He shoveled a heaping dollop of mayo in his mouth as if it were ice cream, and, with mayo seeping from the corners of his lips, turned to my friend and casually asked what movie we were watching. Before she could answer, probably still in shock by what she had just witnessed, I interrupted.

"James are you *seriously* going to eat that mayonnaise straight outta the jar, like its yogurt or something?"

He looked at me like I was crazy for asking such a stupid question. "I got no choice, man. You're fresh out of saltines."

ON ANOTHER OCCASION, when James was walking across the stage at a theatre in Hawaii, he walked into one of our theatrical lights we call "shin lights" which hit him where it hurts the most. And, as he staggered about in intense pain, he fell eight feet into the orchestra pit, directly onto the concrete floor. He somehow managed to climb out of the pit on his own, pale as a ghost from the fall, and said he was going to take it easy for a few minutes.

Yes, that's probably a good idea.

ANOTHER FOND MEMORY of our friend James happened during a baby shower at Jeff and Heidi Bieber's home. In a crowded room, James suddenly gasped loudly, slammed his hand down on his side, squeezed his thigh, and began walking stiff-legged out of the room, explaining dramatically and through clinched teeth that he was having leg cramps. As he was heading out the front door he shouted to his wife Wendy, "Bring me the salt babe, *quick*, bring me the salt shaker off the table."

When she got to him with the salt, he unscrewed the lid and quickly dumped the entire contents of the salt shaker into his hand, then literally threw it into his mouth and began crunching on the salt. Salt got into his nose, ears and hair because of the flurry of his activity. And immediately, while he was still crunching on the pile of salt, he breathed a loud, dramatic sigh of relief, and started nodding his head up and down. When I asked him why in the *world* he was downing so much salt, he looked amazed at my ignorance.

With salt still covering his lips and face and chunks of it still caught between his teeth, he explained it to me by asking me a question. "Tim, why do you think football teams provide salt tablets when it's really hot weather? *He-llo*, because salt fixes cramps, man."

Black, Blue, and Gross All Over

I T SEEMS LIKE ALL PROFESSIONAL ballet dancers enjoy the comforts of hot tubs, whirlpool baths, or any container with hot water in which they can sit and relax. I suppose it soothes their aching muscles. My wife is no exception; she perks up like a dog (a beautiful, classy dog) being offered a treat when she is offered the use of a hot tub. I'm certain the memory I'm about to share has its origin somewhere in West Virginia, and I'm almost certain it was in Wheeling, where we were being hosted by Pastor John Saenger's church.

Our host family was super in every way, and took excellent care of us. It was a timeworn, beautiful house, and the floors, walls, and ceilings were all crafted with a variety of different kinds of richly finished wood. Deana and I remember the family encouraging one of the children to show us their dog doing a trick. The trick was simply how phenomenally high the little rascal could jump. The dog was only about a foot tall at the shoulder, and we witnessed him jumping straight up and touching *their 12 foot ceiling with his nose!* Okay, so that might be off just a smidge; I sometimes get carried away in the retelling of stories. But, he really could jump much higher than either of us had ever seen a dog that small jump. And he could jump high continually—boing-boing-boing. It was hilarious.

It reminds me of another fond memory of a feisty little terrier. Dancer Rick Faucher related to all of us on the bus one morning about having a blast playing "catch" with the resident dog at his homestay earlier that morning. He said the dog never missed the tennis ball—ever. Rick was amused at how tenacious the dog was and began throwing the ball harder and harder in an effort to get it by him, but the determined little critter was hilariously *flawless* in his ability to quickly position himself in front of the approaching ball and crush it to his chest with his two front paws. He would then take a few proud steps toward Rick, dropping the ball on the concrete driveway so that its momentum would cause it to roll toward Rick. Then he would trot back to the spot on the sidewalk, and sort of brace himself, to let Rick know he was ready. He said the dog's body language looked like, "Come on man. Is that the best you got? Come on, try to get it by me!"

Finally Rick hurled it really hard about 5 feet over the dog's head, completely out of reach, even for this canine athlete. The dog raced after the ball to the very end of the driveway which had a little raised lip at the end, and the dog ramped off the end of the driveway and fell out of sight. Rick ran over to the end of the driveway, and to his horror, it was like a small cliff that dropped almost straight down for 40 to 50 feet, and the poor pooch was nowhere in sight. Then the proud little fella appeared, tennis ball clutched firmly in his jaws, as he struggled to climb his way back up the steep embankment to the driveway.

Back to West Virginia. After a great dinner, the host family was excited to bless us for the rest of the evening with the entire upstairs of their beautiful home. What was once a large bedroom had been made into a bathroom, and against the far wall under a window was a gorgeous, old claw-foot bathtub. Deana wasted no time running a piping hot bubble bath while I got little Mathias down for the night in his pop-up crib that had been in over 30 states that year alone. As soon as she got in the tub, she said she felt like a spoiled princess in a castle.

Suddenly, I heard her say, "Oh sick, gross, it's my big toenail, the whole thing fell off. I knew it was coming, I just didn't know when." That was pretty gross, even for me. I was wondering how she knew it would be falling off, no doubt dancing in pointe shoes night after night must have gotten pretty painful at times.

I survived that grotesque toenail encounter, only to forget about the whole ordeal until the next afternoon when we were rolling into Pennsylvania. Deana looked at me with that wide-eyed look as if she had left her purse in a restaurant 200 miles back. When I asked her what was wrong, she was absolutely sick to report that long before she had exited the tub the night before, she put her black and blue big toe nail on the window ledge next to the tub—and forgot to throw it away before we left. Deana was humiliated. How embarrassing it was to know that either the man or woman of the house would find *that* little surprise when they least expected it. Sick! I tried to downplay it by reminding Deana that our hostess was the mother of multiple children, and had seen much grosser things than a toenail. But inwardly, I figured the woman would probably scream when she spotted the giant, discarded, prehistoric-looking toenail. As some of my buddies from high school used to say, "It was sho-nuff gross."

Fast forward four months. The company was warming up for a program at giant Chapel Hill Harvester Church in Atlanta. Deana was on stage, and I was nearby when a couple rushed up to the front of the stage area and shouted, "Hey Tim and Deana! Remember us?" That's not particularly one of our favorite questions because of how often we have zero recollection. We had met *many* people in four months, and stayed in *many* homes. But we both suddenly got the proverbial deer-in-the-headlights expression as soon as they gave us a couple of hints.

"Don't you remember? West Virginia? Your favorite ever claw-foot bath tub?"

Deana imagined she was hearing the theme music from Hitchcock's *Psycho* and wanted to run backstage with embarrassment. But she stood her ground as the man asked his wife to hand him something out of her purse. With a huge smile she excitedly handed him a small jar, like a baby food jar, which, oddly, was full of formaldehyde, and . . . her big toenail. I'm not joking. It was her big toenail. You can't make this stuff up. They were so proud of themselves for preserving it, and for remembering to bring it hundreds of miles south to this church because they had read that Ballet Magnificat would be performing. They couldn't *wait* to show us—it was a treasured prize to them, because they loved us so much. To them it was like an autograph, but way better.

God loves us like that. In fact, he's seen thousands of things in our lives that are way more sickening than that toenail, and yet he still loves us enough to die for us. And thank God he *did* die for us, warts and all.

Baby Shower Prank

A SILLY BUT SINCERE FRIEND of ours named Holly Berry—yes that's her real name—offered to organize a baby shower for my wife. Deana took her up on her offer and was very much looking forward to it. Some dancers from Ballet Magnificat were invited along with an assortment of other friends, and John and Whit Geary opened up their beautiful home for the event.

Before Deana even entered her ninth month of pregnancy, every time we would run into Holly, she would say, "Girl, you *better* not have that baby early, your baby shower is gonna be awesome." And every time, Deana would assure her that she really hoped the baby wouldn't come early, but she didn't have a whole lot of control over that. Then Holly would laugh, and repeat herself, "Just don't let it come early."

The baby came early. But just barely early. The shower was scheduled for a Friday night. The Thursday evening before the shower Deana taught a ballet class, came home and ate dinner, and began having contractions. Baby Miriam was delivered about 3:00 a.m. We had decided to have a home delivery (this doesn't make us super weird— maybe a bit trendy or hipster, before it was cool), so she was born in our bedroom. Deana was in excellent shape, and her doctor thought it would be fine—extremely low risk—for her to deliver at home. We had 5 (yes, *five*) mothers there to assist Deana through the birthing process, and everything was going smoothly until I got involved. We thought it would be memorable if I were allowed to actually deliver the baby, so I was coached and ready.

When the mid-wife and other women thought the delivery was imminent, they suggested I go ahead and get my little plastic surgical gloves on in preparation. I felt my entire body and mind tense up—not because I was about to deliver a baby, but because of the memories kindled when I heard that oh-too-familiar *snap* when I pulled the gloves on. At any rate I was ready now, or so I thought. Just before it was time for her next contraction one of the women said, "Okay Tim, you better go ahead and get some gloves on." I held my hands up to show her that I already had them on. But to my surprise she suggested I had best put another pair on.

It was only then that I noticed. Even though I was thinking I was totally calm, cool, and collected, my gloves belied the fact. All that was left of the glove on my right hand was the part covering my index finger and thumb, and I had "calmly" pulled the *entire* glove on my left hand through all of my fingers, so there was nothing but sort of a blue wristband left. Guess I wasn't as chilled as I thought.

The only other problem was that sweet Miriam had the umbilical cord wrapped around her neck in two places, preventing her from entering the outside world. Thankfully I slipped a finger under the cord and slipped it over her little head and shoulders. But once she was freed from the cord, she popped out so quickly I almost didn't catch her in time. She was crazy beautiful, even from the very beginning.

Deana and Miriam bathed while the women cleaned up the rooms and bed; then they left, and we all fell asleep. The next morning I awoke to Mathias, her four-year-old brother who had slept through the whole thing, waking me up with loud whispers. Wide-eyed and excited to share his discovery with me, he informed me, "Daddy, Daddy. There's some *baby . . . right there,* in *that* crib."

Because there was no anesthesia involved, and because she was in such good shape, and because the Physician lavished grace on her, Deana felt surprisingly good throughout the morning and early afternoon. In fact she was doing so good, I had an idea. I reminded her that the shower was scheduled for that evening at 6:00 p.m., and asked her if she thought she might want to still attend. I assured her that I didn't want to push her if she was too tired. She flashed a big smile, and said that she would like to go, at least for a little while. Convincing her to go was easy, talking her into this next part of the plan was a little more difficult. Well, a *lot* more difficult.

We were (and still are) very close friends with John and Whit Geary, in whose home the shower was to be held. I suggested we show up for the shower a half-hour before anyone else got there, and me "hide" in the very back of the house in the master bathroom with newborn Miriam. Deana could stuff a couple of beach towels under her blouse to give the illusion that she was still with child. When Whit agreed to participate as an accomplice, this pushed Deana over the edge to go through with it.

Co-hostess Holly Berry showed up and commented to Deana right off the bat that she so appreciated Deana waiting to have the baby until after the shower. Deana visited with all of the women for the first 30 minutes or so after everyone had arrived, then whispered to Whit that "it was time." We had coached Whit, and her performance was flawless.

Getting their attention by tapping her spoon on her teacup, she said, "Ladies, there's nothing to be alarmed about, but Deana just stepped to the restroom because she thinks she *may* have just had a contraction. She said it's probably nothing, but I think we should pray for her." After the requisite "oohs" and "ahhs" they all heartily agreed, so Whit led them in prayer for Deana and the baby.

"Dear Lord, thank you so much for sweet Deana and for blessing her and Tim with a second child. We just pray that you'll comfort her right now, and bless her. And Lord if she is going into labor, we would pray that it would be a healthy and speedy delivery. Please comfort her and help her to not be anxious. If it would be your will, we pray she would not have to endure labor nearly so long as she did with Mathias. If she's going into labor we would pray it would be a really easy and quick labor. Amen."

Deana had joined us in the master bath, and as soon as Whit began to pray, Deana, Baby Miriam and I made our way down the hall. We stayed just out of sight of the 25 or so friends, until the instant Whit finished her prayer. Immediately Deana stepped into view, gaining the attention of all the women who were anxious to hear how she was doing, and Deana reached under her blouse and pulled the two beach towels out. The confusion on their faces was priceless, but nothing compared to the next moment when I stepped into view holding newborn Miriam against my chest and facing them. Whit took *two* photographs of one of the women, Leigh McCarty, while her mouth was wide open with confusion and surprise.

I think it was Leigh who asked, "Wait. Who is that baby? Whose baby *is* that? I don't understand."

Deana had been there visiting with them looking nine months pregnant just ten minutes earlier. It was a fun practical joke, but one which probably would have died a miserable death in a different setting, with other friends. Or maybe if Deana had a different husband.

A Royal Flush

I T WAS NOT ONE OF my proudest moments. Okay, well, it was potentially *the* dumbest thing I had ever done in my life. Although it was pretty dumb when I kicked one of my Dad's flip-flops off Lookout Mountain, Tennessee, right after we read on the little plaque that we were so high up on the mountain, we could see objects 20 miles away on a clear day.

I also felt very dopey the time I went into the pastor's office at a Calvary Chapel in Cocoa Beach, Florida. The secretary was typing on the computer with her back to me when I entered. "Hello ma'am." She didn't turn around. I waited for probably 30 seconds, cleared my throat, and said, "Hello there, I'm Tim Dryden." She kept one hand on the keyboard, and raised her other hand with index finger pointing upward, signaling for me to hold my horses. Hmm. These Floridian secretaries are a hardy breed. This time I waited over a minute, and was beginning to bristle. In a firmer tone, and maybe slightly louder, I tried again. "Ma'am I really *do* need to speak to the pastor, it's regarding tonight's program."

Finally, she swiveled around in her chair, but *she* . . . was a *he*. And quite the *he* he was. As it turned out, he was a masculine, handsome man, with a deep voice, and a slight grin because he had purposely tested my patience and knew I would be surprised. After I quit stuttering and we stopped laughing, I proceeded to tell him when during the ballet program that I usually made the appeal for the offering. He said that he would rather just place a basket in the back and not make an appeal for an offering. From experience I knew this never "worked". People simply give more when they are asked. I tried to humbly express this to him, but he just smiled and assured me he would "mention the basket" to his people, and they would respond. It was not easy to submit to his authority and obvious naïveté about offerings.

I was especially concerned in this case because when we had first pulled up to the church to begin unloading and setting up our equipment, the eight men there to help us looked, well, really rough. Some of them were chain smokers, some were cursing, most were dressed shabbily (we almost named one of our daughters Shabbily), and they all were *buried* in tattoos. Granted, none of this disqualifies anyone from being a humble servant, or from being right smack in the middle of the family of God. And they were, to a man, unusually helpful and loving and humble. But, they didn't seem like the types who would fill up a basket set on a table in the back of the room with enough money to meet our need.

I'll just cut to the chase. At that time our need was $2,000 per program, and with only an average number in attendance that evening, they gave almost $3,000, mostly in small bills! So many of them had been rescued from horrific life circumstances by the great Rescuer, and they demonstrated their humility and generosity in ways I'll never forget.

IT WAS PRETTY DUMB of me to ask Dr. Ralph Davis, a brilliant theologian, to read something from his Hebrew Bible to me and several kids in our youth group. Well, actually, that wasn't the dumb part. It was just after the service, and I had boasted about his linguistic brilliance to some of the kids. They wanted to see for themselves that he really could read the Bible in the original language in which it was written. He was very approachable so I explained to him that they wanted to hear for themselves that he could translate. He agreed to our request and asked me what passage I wanted him to read. When I told him it didn't matter, he insisted that I just pick any passage. So I said, "Oh, I don't know, how about the first few verses of Ephesians, chapter 5." The kids waited eagerly. Dr. Davis didn't want to embarrass me, but he reminded me, sort of under his breath, that Ephesians is in the New Testament, which, of course, is translated in Greek not Hebrew. Oh, yeah, my face turned a deep shade of scarlet.

And there was the time my brother had stolen a baseball from a nearby baseball field and threatened to end my life if I told my parents. That day at lunch I casually mentioned that I would like to play baseball that afternoon, and my brother kicked me under the table to warn me not to tattle. "Ouch! I moaned. Why did you have to kick me? I'm not gonna say a word about you stealing the stupid baseball . . . gaah."

Oops.

It was pretty dumb when I swapped some of my peanut M and M's for some of my friend's urine at our annual medical check-up for school sports. He could have had any number of . . . never mind.

Once I had been in a pretty vicious spat with a girl I was dating in my late twenties. When I came home from work there was a card in a big blue envelope lying on top of an Oreo cream pie. *Hah!* I thought. *I knew she'd come to her senses and realize I was right and she was wrong.* As I was removing the plastic wrap and grabbing for a casserole spoon, I thought I should call her in a few minutes and let her know I accept her apology and that everything is okay. But I smiled to myself, and decided I'd let her stew through the night. It would be good for her. And then I took a huge, ravenous bite. And choked. And spit. And gagged. My sweet friend, Charlene Abraham, had filled the pie plate up with shaving cream, and then very carefully crumbled charcoal briquettes all over it for the topping. After I washed my mouth out and coughed and spit and spewed for a few minutes, I opened the card. It was a beautiful card that was imprinted with something like, "I'm so sorry." And she had written below the "I'm so sorry" part, "that I could not have been there to see you choking!" I looked up from the card and thought, "what a jerk." And then it hit me, how did she know I wouldn't read the card first and blow the prank? I continued reading the card. "I knew you wouldn't read the card first because you're a selfish pig, and I knew you'd get one of your stupid giant casserole spoons and take a big bite long before you would read the card."

(That was actually fairly insightful of her).

But those things look smart compared to this last one. We were at a church in central Florida called Carpenter's Home Church, which seated about 8,000 people. It was a gigantic church. We were very fortunate to land a booking at such a large, influential venue. The dancers were inside warming up for a short teaser they would perform for the morning crowd in an effort to draw them back in that night for the full program. I thought I would go out to our bus and clean it up a little, because I had little else to do for at least an hour.

The bus was parked about 80 yards away from the church in the enormous, football stadium sized parking lot. The lot was basically empty because it was so early—it was over an hour before the place would be bustling with cars and people. There was only about half a coffee cup full of "liquid" in our bus toilet, but it would be sitting there in the hot sun all day and could potentially smell up the bus. I say "liquid", because the urine was mixed with this dark turquoise treatment fluid to keep it from having a pungent smell. I hesitated to dump it out in the parking lot because it just seemed kind of, well, gross, but again, it was 80 or 90 yards out away from the church and rain was in the forecast. I thought, *I'm fretting too much about this, what harm is a half of a coffee cup of yuck going to do in this vast parking lot except make a wet spot as big as a dinner plate and evaporate in about 30 minutes?*

So I grabbed the handle and dumped it out onto the parking. There was a problem. A really nasty, *big* problem. I was slightly mistaken as to how much was in the toilet. I had miscalculated by, oh, let's say, 20 gallons.

Yikes!

I had just dumped 20 gallons of nasty stuff into the parking lot of a church early on the Sabbath. By the time I got off the bus to survey the flood, it had found its way to the drainage slopes and had travelled all the way to the church in one gathering, bright, colorful, but beautiful, stream—and in both directions perpendicular to the main stream. An aerial view would have looked like a turquoise cross about the size of a football field.

Yeah, I was feelin' pretty dumb.

The end of this sordid saga has no amusing punchline. I had to admit to the dancers I did something that foolish. Then we all must have carried a total of 75 to 100 five-gallon buckets of water to dump on the "yuck" to dilute it as much as we possibly could and push it to a nearby drainage ditch.

This story would have easily been lost in the dustbin of history, but, for some inexplicable reason, it's one of Keith Thibodeaux's personal favorites, so . . . Keith, this one's for you.

Angels Watching Over Me

B ALLET MAGNIFICAT'S VERY FIRST Christmas program was held in
the 2,300-seat city auditorium in December of 1986. Oddly
enough, there were more dancers then, than at many times through the
company's history. There were four male dancers, the most we've ever
had at any one time.

This would prove to be a very memorable program for both the
audience and the dancers. However, it would probably not be the
dancing or speaking that would be remembered most. It would be
something that happened just prior to the last piece before the
intermission.

A young lady named Judy Fortenberry had graciously accepted
Kathy's offer to sing during the program, allowing the dancers adequate
time for a costume change. She had chosen a current hit song recorded
by Amy Grant, entitled *Angels Watching Over Me*.

As she sang, she glided effortlessly back and forth across the stage.
Her body floated smoothly across the floor. Then, at one point during
the song, her silky steps took her one step too close to the audience as
she sang the lyrics, "Angels watchin' over me, every step I *taaakkee . . .*"

and she fell nearly head first into the orchestra pit, right in front of God and everybody!

Talk about irony.

From the bottom of the pit, a shaky and frail voice cried out pitifully, "Can somebody help me . . . please?" She had managed to hang on to the microphone somehow.

If only we had been filming that year, there's no doubt in my mind we would have won first prize on "America's Funniest Home Videos." Except I guess it didn't happen at home. Whatever. I'm just glad it happened. I mean, I'm not glad she almost hurt herself, but I'm glad it happened, because I love telling stories.

Oh my *goodness!* That reminds me of another story you have to hear. One time we were travelling through the night to our next scheduled performance, and we were rolling through Seattle at 2:30 a.m. and—

My publisher says I gotta stop writing now. Maybe there will be more stories coming soon on my blog. Watch for it—it's called, "All Flimits" (think, "off limits", if that helps).

Bless you!

THE VISTA WAS BREATHTAKING. I was sitting on a balcony of a gorgeous log home on the side of a picturesque North Carolina mountain. Our gracious host extended an invitation to me to stay for a few days and begin writing. Of the 800+ homes in which we had been hosted through the years, this gorgeous log home was our absolute favorite. The director and film crew of *The Last of the Mohicans* had requested the use of the home, but were declined the opportunity during the filming of that movie because some were smokers.

Many people throughout the country had encouraged me to record some of the hilarious—and amazing—things we experienced as we traveled around this great nation. It was time. Following are the first words I wrote on a borrowed laptop:

> *Here I am, a dream finally realized—it's quiet at least temporarily, I have the advantage of a computer that works, coffee in my veins, traffic in my brains, and a blank palette— the genesis of everything that's anything called art, whether tremendous or trash.*

As I fondly remember that beautiful morning and recording that first stream of consciousness, I see the terms "dream", "palette", and "art" and can't help but get excited. It is *still* my dream that the Artist in me will brush these stories on the palette of many lives on which he is skillfully painting even now.

My goals for writing this book were—and remain—three-fold. First, I hope my five precious children, three of whom weren't yet born at the time these stories unfolded, will laugh, learn, and love these memories. Second, it's my prayer that in some way you will be tangibly encouraged and that you will laugh out-loud as you read these pages. And, most importantly, I hope this work meets the approval of the Artist in me, and will cause many to see clearly how magnificent and masterful is the living Creator of creativity, the Artist.

Finally, I sincerely hope I make *buckets* of money from the publication of this book. The publisher has assured me that if I write and call my parents, harass my in-laws, and pester everyone on social media, there's a good chance we might just sell *at least* 15-20 copies in the first few years alone. Move over, "Little Ricky".

Made in the USA
Charleston, SC
24 November 2015